Peter Conrad

Peter Conrad was born in Ho[...] a Rhodes Scholarship. In 19[..] [...] was made a Fellow of All Souls College, and since 1973 has taught English literature at Christ Church, Oxford. He is a Fellow of the Royal Society of Literature, and an Honorary Fellow of the Australian Academy of the Humanities. His many books include *Down Home: Revisiting Tasmania* and *At Home in Australia* (based on the photographic collection of the National Gallery in Canberra); he has also written *Modern Times, Modern Places, Cassell's History of English Literature*, and – most recently – studies of Alfred Hitchcock and Orson Welles. He is a feature writer and reviewer for *The Observer*. He lives in London and New York.

Boyer Lectures

Each year the ABC invites a prominent Australian to present the result of his or her work and thinking on major social, scientific or cultural issues in a series of radio talks known as the Boyer Lectures. The series was inaugurated in 1959 under the title of ABC Lectures, but in 1961 was renamed as a memorial to the late Sir Richard Boyer who, as chairman of the ABC had been one of those responsible for its introduction.

The Boyer Lectures are broadcast each year on ABC Radio National's 'Big Ideas' program.

ABC Radio National is available throughout Australia on 260 transmitters including:

Adelaide 729AM
Brisbane 792AM
Canberra 846AM
Darwin 657AM
Gold Coast 90.1FM
Hobart 585AM
Melbourne 621AM
Newcastle 1512AM
Perth 810AM
Sydney 576AM

For your local frequency go to the ABC Radio National website at abc.net.au/rn or call 1300 13 9994 during working hours.

For ABC Radio National broadcast times and program details go to abc.net.au/rn or call listener enquiries on 02 8333 2821 during working hours.

Tales of Two Hemispheres
Boyer Lectures 2004

Tales of Two Hemispheres

Boyer Lectures 2004

Peter Conrad

ABC
Books

Published by ABC Books for the
AUSTRALIAN BROADCASTING CORPORATION
GPO Box 9994 Sydney NSW 2001

Copyright © Peter Conrad 2004

First published December 2004

All rights reserved. No part of this publication may be reproduced, stored in a retrieval system or transmitted in any form or by any means, electronic, mechanical, photocopying, recording or otherwise, without the prior written permission of the Australian Broadcasting Corporation.

ISBN 0 7333 1515 1.

Text and cover concept designed by Reno Design Group
Cover designed by Christabella Designs
Typeset in 11/18pt ITC Cushing by Kirby Jones
Printed and bound in Australia by Griffin Press, Adelaide

5 4 3 2 1

Contents

one
Antipodes 1

two
Austrailure 18

three
Down Under 35

four
Up Over 52

five
Austerica 69

six
Oz 87

appendices 107
1. *'How to Like this Place'* 109
2. *Thirty-six Views of Mount Wellington* 135

acknowledgments 163

one
Antipodes

As soon as we become conscious and curious, we struggle to locate ourselves in the world, and if possible to tether ourselves to it. I remember the first time I realised how much trouble I was going to have with this business of mental anchorage. I was on my way home from school in Hobart during the 1950s, gazing up at a sky that might have been an inverted, unfathomable ocean. Its height seemed more like depth, which made me feel dizzy. Could I be walking upside down? I was trying to make sense of the globe, to whose underside we supposedly clung; though I didn't yet know it, Australians inhabited a fantastical region known as the Antipodes. The word meant that our feet were opposite—opposed, that is, to those who triumphantly bestrode the world because they had the good fortune to be born in the northern hemisphere, where the maps were made.

Back then, I did not feel attached to the ground beneath my own feet. My head floated off like a wayward balloon, carried along by the English books I read. In 1968 my body followed, thanks to one of those scholarships dreamed up by Cecil Rhodes to give boys from the imperial backblocks an 'instruction in life and manners'. It was a long while before I looked back. But eventually I did peer around the curvature of the earth in quest of a land that is a synonym for the alluring, baffling idea of the south, since the imagination summed up a Terra Australis long before any southern continent was discovered.

Ancient geographers like Ptolemy presumed that such a place existed, postulating a *terra incognita* that served as an antipodal ballast to their northern land mass. We had the honour to be a pedestal, or a footstool. The very notion of a division into hemispheres implied inequity, conflict. Plato imagined that the first beings were shaped like globes, symbols of full-bodied wholeness. A jealous god smashed them in half, and ever since the opposites—like north and south, male and female, or the yolk and white of an egg—have been trying to recover their original, peaceful interdependence. That myth at least gave us hope of reunion with our other halves. Christianity, on the other hand, denied that there could be any such happy ending; it disapproved, as St Augustine put it, of 'the fable that there are Antipodes', because the very existence of such a place queried the universality of the religion headquartered in Rome. If southerners existed, they couldn't be descendants of Adam, and consequently wouldn't suffer from original sin or require divine redemption. It was theologically tidier to assume that the bottom of our mundane sphere was a wilderness of water or sand. But

Australia's official nonentity did not prevent people from speculating about what it might be like. Usually they assumed that it must be Europe standing on its head, which made it a satire on the moral topsy-turvydom of their own society. Sir Thomas Browne called the fool 'Antipodes unto the wise', and the Elizabethan clergyman Joseph Hall wrote about a fantastical voyage to Terra Australis Incognita, where he explored the regions of Fooliana and Theevingen.

Early in the seventeenth century, the Portuguese sea-captain Pedro Fernández de Quirós tried to persuade King Philip III of Spain to annex the southland he mistakenly thought he had discovered. Hoping for royal favour, he named this territory Austrialia del Espíritu Santo. The neologism Austrialia was courtly pun, underlining Spain's alliance with the imperial house of Austria. In fact Quirós had stumbled onto an island in what are now known as the New Hebrides, supposedly an upside-down equivalent of Scotland: the naming of Antipodean places was a competition between mismatched metaphors. In his petition, Quirós adapted the idea of the opposed feet for his own purposes. The world, he assured the monarch, was a body, with Spain as its controlling head, and the new colony might be imagined not as its foot but as its fingernail. To be antidigital is an improvement, I suppose, on being Antipodean; hands are more closely wired to the brain than feet.

As the known world's vanishing point, Australia licensed the wishful thinking of those who wanted to redesign nature and embellish miserable reality. A fictional journal was published in 1797, passed off as a record of La Pérouse's expedition to Botany Bay. It described noble savages playing oboes and amorously frolicking in tropical glades. Maps of the world, as Oscar Wilde said, must leave room for Utopia. For the romantic dreamer who forged that journal, the good place was Australia, situated as far as possible from cynical Europe.

The idyll did not last for long. Though maps may leave Utopian blanks, they are drawn up to regiment space, and to demonstrate how power radiates out from the centre to the periphery. On a round earth, space should be egalitarian, with no beginning or end, no up or down. But lines of latitude and longitude transform the globe into a cage or a cell. Voyages of discovery in the southern hemisphere catalogued novelties and claimed ownership, but they also briskly discounted the value of the new possessions. During the 1820s, Thomas Hervey, a pompous and untalented versifier, referred to the Pacific as a 'liquid waste', which makes it sound like sewage. He also called Australia a 'chimera', the word applied by classical authors to unclassifiable monsters. Captain Cook was for Hervey the 'northern Oedipus', with Australia as the sphinx whose riddle he solved. The sphinx expired when Oedipus demystified her; Hervey perhaps wished that Australia, having once been sighted, would discreetly vanish again.

The Antipodes were the body's extremities, its feet or its fingernails. British geography emphasised another correspondence, and saw Australia as a sphincter. In 1865 Henry Kingsley called it a 'scentless cesspool for a vast quantity of nameless rubbish'—scentless because far away, so its ordure didn't vex the nostrils of Victorian Britons, and nameless because the excreted convicts had no right to individual identity. Even if we weren't treated as an unsightly anus, we were still relegated to the globe's hind quarters. Joseph Banks, contrasting the terrain of Australia's east coast with the lush Indies, likened it to 'the back of a lean cow'. Banks couldn't resist anatomising the poor ragged balding beast in woebegone detail: 'Where her scraggy hip bones have stuck out farther than they ought', knocks and abrasions had 'intirely bard them of their share of covering'. Just think for a moment of the cliffs outside Sydney—a porous honeycomb above a cobalt sea: how could anyone have seen this landscape as a scuffed cow?

The violence of such language registered a metaphysical dread. A northern world that considered itself complete, perfected, made in the deity's own image, was shocked when it came across another model of creation. Could Australia be the handiwork of God's enemy, the mad demiurge described by Gnosticism? The unknown looked abnormal, grotesquely warped. Seen through eyes trained by the Enlightenment to categorise familiar species, the kangaroo and platypus were as alarming as extraterrestrials. Indeed Charles de Brosse, in the history of navigation he published in 1756, described Australian marsupials as Martians, strays from 'another planet'. Throughout the nineteenth century, thinkers struggled to reconcile Australia's eccentric flora and fauna with the law-abiding habits of northern species. Down here, trees shed their bark not their leaves, and animals—rather than preferring the privacy of the womb—deposited their young in an external pouch. Why weren't nature's edicts universal? More was at stake than mere taxonomic tidiness; ultimately, the problem was theological. God's survival depended on harmonising the hemispheres. When biologists abandoned the effort, the monopolistic creator who formed the earth in Genesis had no choice but to die.

Australia could only be explained as God's fumbling rehearsal or his spiteful afterthought. In 1820 a contributor to the *Edinburgh Review* suggested that Botany Bay must have been nature's 'first essay in making continents': a trial run, and a botched job. Barron Field, writing a poem about the kangaroo in 1819, could only imagine that the beast was pieced together 'on Creation's holiday', a saturnalian respite after the hard work of shaping the northern hemisphere was done. Or perhaps it might be what Field called an 'afterbirth', like an extruded, disposable placenta. He meant that it was 'not conceiv'd in the Beginning' but after 'the first sinning'. When man fell, God punished his former pet for disobedience by returning to earth to invent some new creatures; the animals of this second generation were monsters, designed to frighten Adam and his offspring. This made the kangaroo a marsupial bogeyman. Later, according to fundamentalists, that same vindictive God swilled away the misbegotten Antipodes in a deluge. Botanists couldn't understand why eucalypts grew nowhere else in the world; the correct doctrinal answer was that they had all been submerged by Noah's flood. Even so, Mark Twain cheekily wondered why that the platypus wasn't mentioned in the inventory of creatures Noah ushered onto the ark. For him, that proved the truth of evolutionary theory. Darwin's landfall in Sydney and Hobart in 1836 made him wonder if the Christian deity had a more prankish, irregular rival in the southern hemisphere. 'Surely,' he whispered in his diary, 'two separate creators must have been at work', with the equator acting as a border between their different realms. The evidence of Australia disputed God's workmanship; the idea of creation gave way to a long, slow history of hybridising and metamorphosis.

Hidden on the world's nether side, Australia was literally an underworld. Hal Porter examined the antipodal illogic of the penal colony in his novel *The Tilted Cross*, set in Van Diemen's Land during the 1840s. Porter's Hobart skulks beneath a starry crucifix that has tilted sideways. The town is a shoddy copy of London seen in a distorting mirror, which reverses the scale of social esteem. Its East End lies to the north, while the West End is southerly. The builders of Georgian mansions positioned their windows to face south, as in England; they deprived themselves of light rather than acknowledge that, down here, the sun shone from the north. No wonder I scratched my head when I tried to orient myself a century later. In another novel about those grim beginnings, Thomas Keneally's *The Playmaker*, the hero calls the bereft and sterile continent a 'convict moon', the deathly antithesis of the bright, life-giving sun. It's a wicked libel, because actually we get the sun first. But that is the bequest of colonial cosmology: it left us feeling estranged from a world that we saw from the wonkiest and lowliest of angles.

Even the lunar analogy is a reminder of our exclusion, back then, from the orderly normality of nature. When the novelist Christopher Koch got to London in the 1950s, he scrutinised the bleary, sodium-tinted night sky above the city and realised with a shock that 'the moon in Australia was upside down'. The cratered O that is supposed to be the mouth of the man in the moon is actually, from Australia's vantage point, one of his eyes, or perhaps a hole drilled between them. Because of this skewed world-view, the fairy tales that project human faces into outer space couldn't work their charm for Australian children. During his visit to Australia in 1897, Mark Twain had breezily and almost blasphemously noticed that the sacred reading of the Antipodean heavens made no sense. The Southern Cross, he observed, was in need of repair. He couldn't see the analogy with a crucifix, and thought that the random pinpricks of light looked more like a coffin or a kite. Now that the English-speaking races had taken over management of the globe, he suggested they should re-organise the stars. Why not rename the constellation that we wrongly think of as our protective canopy, and call it the Southern Kite? The 'general emptiness' of a godless firmament, he joked, is the proper place for kites not crosses.

When Nellie Melba came home to 'sing 'em muck' in 1902, she paid a visit to Melbourne University. A star-struck professor greeted her, and made a speech in which he flattered Melba by extinguishing Australia—a 'remote, quiet, isolated nook of the universe' as he called it, through whose 'silent heaven' the expat soprano had flashed 'like some northern comet'. Asteroids, he assumed, could only originate in the north; after Melba's transit was over, the south would revert to inky obscurity. Meanwhile, in what the grovelling academic described as 'this immature, ... unintellectual city', Melbourne's prodigal daughter blazed like 'the presence of that occult divine power which in higher states of civilisation is openly worshipped'. This is less a cringe than an act of total abasement. If the Virgin Mary had hovered into view above the quadrangle on a pink cloud, she'd have been welcomed with the same slavish piety.

It's lucky that Australians are nihilistic humourists: one way of overcoming our disgrace was to take a rough pride in living in a land that was literally Godforsaken, disowned by the Anglican creator. A traveller in a Somerset Maugham story makes a detour to Thursday Island after being 'told ... in Sydney that it was the last place God ever made'. Being a naive Pom, he doesn't realise that the comment is not a recommendation. Perhaps such travellers deserved to be misled, because their main purpose in touring Britain's remote possessions was to remind themselves how much better off they were at home. Those of us whose world they dismissively passed through could only feel ashamed of our toehold on the globe and our topographical absurdity. At worst we were upside down, at best back to front. Agatha Christie, accompanying her husband on a trade mission in 1922, at least varied the customary complaint about the bush. English trees had 'dark trunks and light leafy branches'; the trunks of the eucalypts were silvery, their leaves darker, so the landscape resembled 'the negative of a photograph'. The positive image belonged in England, so we inhabited a spookily immaterial negation. Even the drains derided us. After a soothing soak in a tub of pine crystals, the murderous Tasmanian heroine of Helen Hodgman's novel *Blue Skies* watches the water 'whirl all my sins away down the plughole. Anti-clockwise, of course.' The second sentence registers a qualm: does the purifying magic of the bath water work this way round?

Between the hemispheres a Manichean battle was fought, a war of light and dark. I'm reminded of this whenever, on flights to or from Australia, I find myself spending the doped, immobile hours with my eyes fixed on the video map: here you can see the plane boring its way round the world as the border between day and night shifts like a moving vertical equator, brightening one continent while decreeing that gloom has to settle on another. The British politicians who devised the policy of transportation believed they had the monopoly of rational daylight, and thought of Australia as a benighted, morally murky place. But the little electronic map on the plane shows that light and dark actually chase each other round in a relativistic, inconclusive circle. Mr Brown in Patrick White's *The Solid Mandala* quits sooty England so that his sons can be 'reared in the light of an empty country'. He is delighted to think that 'there aren't any shadows in Australia'. Such optimism infuriated White himself, who—because Australia wasn't shadowy enough—set off to travel in the other direction. Wherever you are, light and dark alternate; like all opposites, they are mutually dependent. In a letter in 1981 White remarked that he and his bossy mother were so much alike that they could not be in the same room without squabbling. Therefore, during his period of exile in London or New York, he 'chose to live in another hemisphere' from the one she inhabited. It was a drastic but ineffectual gesture. You can hardly banish your shadow to the Antipodes, because it's inseparable from yourself.

When I first read Nevil Shute's *On the Beach*, what dismayed me was the sentence of nuclear death imposed on Australia. Was this, I wondered in the late 1950s, all I had to look forward to? Would I grow up just in time to die? Re-reading the novel forty years later, I found something in it that's even more depressing: the plaintive implication that no-one in Australia had ever been more than half alive, even before the contentious nations of the other hemisphere cooked up their fatal war. The heroine Moira wonders why we should have to die. (This is the role Ava Gardner was imported to play in the film, since in those days we were not permitted to be ourselves.) No bombs exploded below the equator; Moira thinks that our relegation to the end of the earth must guarantee immunity. Dwight, the worldly-wise American submarine commander, puts her right. Though winds don't blow across the equator, that doesn't make it a sanitary cordon; the winds carrying the radiation sickness obey a pressure equator that shifts seasonally. Moira had planned a trip to the destination she piningly calls 'home'. Now she is doomed to die without having seen the northern hemisphere—which means that she has hardly lived at all. She laments that she will never get to the Rue de Rivoli, and she's unprepared to accept the 'Paris end' of Collins Street as a substitute.

Dwight pities her and all her benighted compatriots. He is less indulgent when they go to an exhibition of religious art that depicts the Armageddon they are living through. He derides the muddled terrain in a painting of incinerated Manhattan. The Brooklyn Bridge has been placed on the New Jersey side, and the Empire State Building is plonked down in the middle of Central Park. A down-under artist inevitably gets things back to front. It would not have occurred to the incompetent, untravelled painter to imagine what Sydney might look like as a necropolis. Shute's novel assumes that the world began in the upper hemisphere and will also end there. Australia, lasting a few extra months, merely adds a brief, frustrated epilogue to human history. The bang (to paraphrase TS Eliot, from whom Shute took his title) was in the north. All the south can do is whimper.

Antipodes

The fearful future which Shute predicted during my childhood is now the remote past. The world is still dangerous, but it also smaller—abridged by faster and more frequent travel, further unified by electronic technologies that seek to eliminate space altogether. West and east remain at odds, but north and south know each other better, so there is no excuse for their disdainful ignorance or our craven awe. Geographically the very notion of the Antipodes has long been obsolete since, of course, the continents above the equator don't need a counterweight below to keep the globe from toppling sideways into deep space. But the myth retains its appeal, even though the tales the hemispheres tell about each other are now less recriminatory. Christopher Koch once wrote an essay about the idea of the 'lost hemisphere', which described our Jungian quest to be reunited with our tantalising other half. For him this effort to match Australia's spirit with 'the spirit of the ancestral land in his head' was 'the task of a lifetime'. Koch's lost hemisphere was of course the northern one; we were still the losers, the homesick seekers on pilgrimages to Europe with its castles and cathedrals. Nowadays you're now more likely to find the north lamenting its loss of the southern hemisphere. We have become the beguiling object of desire for legions of European back-packers who are quite happy to leave their history behind. What land has a more primordial ancestry than Australia?

These new northern pilgrims are less snooty than their colonising predecessors. They react with wonder and envy to a world that is not yet befouled, congested, irredeemably humanised. The naturalist David Attenborough remembers taking up position in a hide near Nourlangie Rock in Kakadu so he could spy on some magpie geese. He noticed that he was crouching in an attitude of reverence, as if the South Alligator River were 'a holy place' (which of course it is). The grazing geese, so unflustered, made him feel that it must have been 'like this before man appeared on earth'. And when the Australian Adam does appear on that earth, he seems to belong to a new species, an improvement on the worn-out European prototype or the robotised American model. This is how Australians looked to the sibylline travel writer Jan Morris in the 1980s. Watching some children on skateboards in an Adelaide park, she recalled Crèvecoeur's announcement exactly two centuries before that Americans were humanity relaunched, new men who entertained new ideas and acted on new principles. The fooling and raillery of the Australian kids, their relaxed gait and the drawling languor of their speech, their indifference to ethnic quarrels—all this convinced Morris that she was watching a blithe new stage in the evolution of the human race.

Perhaps a further mutation was marrying these people to the species with which they shared the land. A male and a female cop on horseback in the park, 'both of supernal handsomeness', made Morris catch her breath. She couldn't stop herself imagining them without their uniforms: undressed, she suspected, they might be 'actually marsupial'. I know what she meant. When I saw Hugh Jackman as Peter Allen in *The Boy from Oz* on Broadway, he reminded me of a hyper-kinetic, disco-dancing kangaroo. There's another piece of evidence in a photograph from William Yang's chronicle of high and low society in Sydney during the 1980s. It shows the rear ends of three faceless tribal braves whose turf is the gay bars of Oxford Street. Gathered for a sweaty corroboree, they have redefined national icons as sexual fetishes. Two of them wear the map on their vests: the country is a jungle of fur growing from a skin of leather—this is Australia in the raw. Kangaroos with pronged, priapic tails vault through the air above the Torres Strait on their waistcoats, and koalas happily manacled together by non-onerous chains dangle from their belts. The shorts of the third man are a different proposition. He too is wearing the map, outlined in black on white cotton. But this time the contours of the continent are streamlined, jazzily inflected. Cape York could have been scribbled in by an excited needle registering the tempo of the heart, and Tasmania tapers into an arrow that points to the cleft of his buttocks.

St Augustine was right to be worried by the idea of the Antipodes. Creatures like Morris's centaurs or Yang's sleek urban savages hardly qualify as fallen men, and they lie outside the church's prim jurisdiction. In 1829 the romantic radical Edward Gibbon Wakefield, who never got to Australia, imagined Botany Bay as 'the earthly paradise'. Not Christianity's Eden, which was given to men and then censoriously debarred; for Wakefield, Australia's latitude made it a pagan place. Sydney, he pointed out, was the Antipodean equivalent of Paphos, 'where Adonis was conceived, and where the Goddess of Beauty had two temples'. The same analogy occurred to the photographer Max Dupain in 1935, when he received an invitation from Norman Lindsay, the notorious high priest of vitalism and erotic liberty. Lindsay lived in the Blue Mountains, but for Dupain it was like being summoned to Delphi, where Apollo's worshippers gathered.

It's good that Australia is no longer cast as the northern hemisphere's notion of hell. Still, we need to be wary about what kind of heaven we flatter ourselves that we live in. The figures Max Dupain photographed had exemplary classical physiques, like his 'Sunbaker', but despite the homage to Greece, they also disturbingly resembled the eugenic statuary of Germany during the Third Reich. Do we inhabit a paradise of brainless, soulless, sun-tanned flesh? Dupain's son Rex, registering his doubts, has photographed his own versions of his father's iconic scenes, and shown that Australians are multi-coloured people of all shapes and sizes, not white, idealised acolytes of Venus and Adonis. Old blokes in swimming trunks do stretching exercises beside the angular Opera House in a photograph Rex Dupain calls 'Cubist Morning': the building may be abstract, but the saggy bodies are not. In other photographs, Lebanese bathers enjoy the democratic water at Bondi, and a little boy whose family comes from India proudly flaps an Australian flag to celebrate the centenary of Federation.

For Rex Dupain, the beach is not a strenuous gymnasium, as it was for his father. Instead, as he says, it delivers 'a sense of well-being and peace', the result of 'gazing away from your feet at the water's edge to the horizon line and on into infinity'. Note how he aligns the feet in his comment: stretched on a bed of sand, they extend towards that dazzling infinity. We are only Antipodean if we remain upright, pointing through the earth's centre at those who stand on the other side with their feet opposed to ours. The old antipodal world worked along a vertical axis, discriminating between top and bottom. The world we are lucky enough to live in now is globular. When we take the weight off, we wrap ourselves around its gently bent contours and float towards the horizon.

Late in the seventeenth century, the poet Andrew Marvell pictured Antipodeans wearing shoes on their heads. He was right in a way: for too long we behaved as if our brains were lodged in our boots, which we used to excavate a short cut up to another hemisphere that was never home. To us, after all, Europe and America are the Antipodes. Let's turn the world upside down and see what it looks like.

two
Austrailure

Puns don't work on the radio: you need to see the way a word is spelled in order to recognise that it's being put to a dualistic use. But the pun I have in mind is inescapable, because it sums up the legacy of self-disbelief Australia had to cast off. It's a joke, though it is also shocking, almost unspeakable. Ours is a country whose name can be rhymed with failure.

Australia was identified in anticipation, before it was assigned an exact location on the map, even before anyone knew whether the fanciful southland actually existed. The prophetic word evoked an idea, and was an invitation to fantasise—just as, in the tourist brochures or on posters in the acrid gusty tunnels of the London Underground, it still is. Because it was an illusory notion, it could be flexed in order to conjure up other dreamy destinations, as when Quirós re-spelled it Austrialia so as to incorporate the Austria of the Hapsburg emperors. For poets, the word was awkward. It made them stammer, as Walter Murdoch discovered when he adjudicated a state competition for patriotic

Austrailure

odes. He admired the bard whose salutation faced up to the dangerous rhyme:

> Hail, beauteous land! hail, bonzer West Australia;
> Compared with you, all others are a failure.

But he also acknowledged the diplomatic problem, which provoked another entrant to invert the state's name:

> Hail, Groperland! Australia West!
> Of earth's fair places thou art best.

Vivian Smith risks the rhyme in a satire about a man of letters whose career begins with a book of poems that 'passed in the Antipodes for Art'. Smith's character then devotes himself to self-publicising, and blames the country for stunting his talent. When he finally publishes some more poems, the literary community reacts with polite cowardice:

> Of course we all agreed we would be kind,
> haunted by our own sense of deeper failure.
> It's human not to keep your standards high.
> We need his type of person in Australia.

That's the end of Smith's poem, drawlingly venomous but also self-scourging.

The rhyme is scarring, like the mark of a brand, and it encapsulates the scorn that underlay the colonial occupation. Hence its use by Barron Field, who—after a mediocre legal career in England—got appointed as a judge of the New South Wales Supreme Court. In his spare time, he promoted himself as an 'Austral Harmonist', and in 1819 published a book called *First Fruits of Australian Poetry*. He thought Australia 'unpicturesque, unmusical', though he did eloquently compliment one local animal:

> Kangaroo, Kangaroo!
> Thou Spirit of Australia,
> That redeems from utter failure,
> From perfect desolation
> … this fifth part of the Earth.

Much as Field wanted to say that Australia was not a failure, he found it hard to convince himself. He accuses the kangaroo of the same ugly asymmetry exhibited by his couplets: he desperately rhymes 'poetical' with 'chimeras all', or 'camel-wise' with 'panther size'. The words don't belong together because the different parts of the kangaroo—a camel's head and a panther's hindquarters—don't cohere, so Field blames the animal for the faults of his own awful verse. His kangaroo is a mixture of metaphors, an anatomical match for the verbal muddle that Horace deplored in his Latin treatise on poetry. Horace warned writers against grafting together inconsistent images, which, he said, was like sticking a man's head on a horse's neck or giving a woman's torso the nether parts that ought to belong to a fish. But hadn't the creator of the southern hemisphere ignored these rules of proportionality and decorum? Field diagnosed the kangaroo as a cross between a squirrel and a deer, with five claws on its forepaw but only three talons on its hind legs, as if it were partly avian (though it did its hopping with its tail). At the end of his poem, manufacturing false rhymes on words with feminine endings, he assures the kangaroo that

> ... howsoe'er anomalous,
> Thou art not yet incongruous,
> Repugnant or preposterous.

But after this pile-up of patter, the best he can do is to accept that the poor creature is incorrigible:

> Thou can'st not be amended: no;
> Be as thou art; thou best art so.

At least Field generously gave the kangaroo permission to go on existing. Joseph Banks, collecting specimens at Botany Bay in 1770, went botanising with his musket. 'I made a small excursion,' Banks said, 'in order to shoot anything I could meet with.' That included a kangaroo, which he called 'a mouse-coloured greyhound'. Animals like this—or Field's 'sooty swans' and 'duck-moles' (which is how he characterised the platypus)—offended the preconceptions of both botany and poetry, and anything that could not be classified deserved to be killed. The same rule applied to the continent's human inhabitants. The pirate William Dampier, making a landfall near Melville Island late in the seventeenth century, called its natives 'the miserablest people in the world', indistinguishable from brutes: failures, in Field's terms, who did not merit redemption. We can only recognise or comprehend what we think we already know, so when Banks arrived almost a century later he trained his telescope on the coast and spotted figures who looked 'enormously black'. He admitted that he'd been so prejudiced by Dampier's account that he and his crew 'fancied we could see their colour when we could scarce distinguish whether or not they were men'. But that too was a proviso licensing violence, or at least dismissal. When Banks got closer, he saw that the Aboriginal women 'did not copy our mother Eve even to the fig leaf'. Fortunately, this meant that he was unrelated to them. If Eve was not their mother, they could be expelled from the human family and morally disowned, like the new country's unintelligible, miscegenated fauna.

Such commentaries afflicted Australia with a burden of original sin. The kangaroo was literally scapegoated, as were Banks's Aboriginal women—as indeed we all were, until we began to repudiate the charge that we were miscreants. Field denied that the roo was created by a God who 'bless'd His work at first,/ And saw that it was good', because no-one could smile approvingly on the haphazardly assembled beast. By the end of the nineteenth century, thanks to Darwin, the creative force shifted away from God to the evolutionary striving of nature itself. But when this

Austrailure

happened, the condemnation of backward Australia was simply rephrased. In 1903 Frank Baker, superintendent of the zoo in Washington DC, declared that our marsupials were 'the stupidest animals in the world'. He condemned them because they had not developed predatory American habits and turned into social Darwinians. They had no enemies to fight, and no need to forage for food; hence their retardation. Baker unregretfully wrote off the Tasmanian tiger, which belonged, he said, 'to a race of natural-born idiots'. Luckily the thylacine was virtually extinct, otherwise euthanasia might have been prescribed, as it was by the Nazis with their mercy killings of those they considered to be cretins.

Even jokes could be offensive and wounding. In Oscar Wilde's play *Lady Windermere's Fan* a venal London duchess is hoping to marry her daughter to a rich young man from Sydney, whose father cans food that even the servants in the ducal house refuse to eat. Though she needs his money, she reserves the right to patronise his homeland. With what's meant to be cutting hauteur, she says she has heard that Australia is a young country. Mr Hopper smartly contradicts her. It was made, he drawls, at the same time as all the others. Later she tries to make small talk about kangaroos, though she's still perplexed by them. Do they fly about or crawl? Are they pretty or horrid? Another Wildean dandy in *The Importance of Being Earnest* is threatened with deportation, and shrills 'Australia! I'd rather die.' He's then warned that he must choose between this world, the next or Australia, which is perhaps the netherworld. 'Oh, well!' he sighs. 'The accounts I have received of Australia and the next world are not particularly encouraging.' As it happened, Wilde himself chose not to flee abroad when he had the chance, and was sentenced to two years in Reading gaol. Australia would have been a better choice.

The northerners kept up their campaign of disparagement until very recently, not even sparing innocent fowls. During a visit to Tasmania in 1940, the British balletomane Arnold Haskell cast a quizzical eye on a native hen, which he had the effrontery to describe as 'rather ridiculous'. This mockery of wildlife was extended to cover other native specimens. Americans would indignantly object if anyone said that armadillos and gophers were deformed and grotesque. All the same, in December 1959 Robert Mitchum lumped Australians together with their marsupials and scornfully wrinkled his lazy lip at the lot of them. Mitchum had spent a few weeks brushing away blowflies and equally pesky journalists around Port Augusta, where he was playing an Australian drover in the film of Jon Cleary's *The Sundowners*; in Sydney, as he boarded the plane back to Los Angeles, a child stopped him and asked for his autograph. This is what he wrote: 'In a country which regards with casual aplomb the anachronism of the kangaroo and the platypus, the being homo sapiens is a disgusting oddity. Merry Christmas, Bob Mitchum.'

After the fauna, Australia's flora came in for criticism. This is surely one of the oddest episodes in the history of man's vexed relationship with nature: our trees were chided for bad manners or reviled for what seemed to be incurable neuroses, and all because they had the misfortune not to belong to English species. No wonder those same libelled trees now receive consoling hugs from greenies! In 1843 a character in Charles Rowcroft's *Tales of the Colonies* repeated the conventional argument that the southern hemisphere was the creator's clumsy apprentice work, its mistakes rectified on 'the other side'. No 'decent, respectable tree in England', as he put it, would behave so improperly, shedding its bark, not its leaves, and letting the tattered remnants hang in rags. Australia was expected to be an outdoor drawing-room, with vegetation patterned like wallpaper. HM Hyndman, who visited in the 1870s, described the trees even more unkindly. He regarded the blue gums as dipsomaniac ghouls, so 'dissipated-looking' with their 'blotchy trunks' that 'Dante could well have represented them in his *Inferno*, in the shape of drunken men … standing around in sempiternal penance of their orgies'. This is not quite what Ruskin called the pathetic fallacy, that conviction of fellow feeling between men and nature; it's more like the demonic fallacy. Koalas are supposed to get tipsy on the fermented juice of the gum leaves they chew, but it's another matter altogether to accuse the trees of being drunkards and then damn them to hell for their crimes. I'm surprised that Hyndman didn't also attack them for being blue. In *Postcards from Surfers*, Helen Garner recalls the scandalised reaction of a Brazilian friend in Paris to whom she showed a reproduction of a Streeton landscape, one of the votive icons on a homesick altar in her bedroom. He looked at it and said

Tales of Two Hemispheres

'Les arbres sont rouges?' The trees are red? How dare they be? No other colonised country had to cope with such a handicap: we were taught to despise our own landscape.

Nevil Shute's characters in *On the Beach* still deferentially ask a foreigner's permission to admire Australian nature, whose beauty is of course relative to that of the northern hemisphere. Moira's family lives on a property ten miles inland from Port Phillip Bay; her mother tells their American guest that the area is 'nice', though 'it can't compare with England' (where she has set foot just once). When Dwight politely praises their surroundings, Moira begs for extra reassurance: 'Is it as beautiful as places in America or England? ... One sort of thinks that everything in England or America must be much better. That this is all right for Australia, but that's not saying much.' Perhaps Dwight's generosity is prompted by the sight of some oaks and maples, which remind him of the northern hemisphere. Until now the only trees he has seen are wattles and eucalypts, which don't merit a compliment.

Shute's prose is hardly capable of validating the local flora, let alone celebrating it. His writing remains as bland as a real estate brochure. He refers tautologously to 'a pastoral view over undulating pastures and coppices', or casually glances at 'a country of gracious farms on undulating hilly slopes ... where well kept paddocks were interspersed with coppices and many trees'. Pastoral pastures? Coppices, many trees? In the 1950s our love of the land still dared not speak its name, because it lacked a

Austrailure

language in which to do so. The scenic vocabulary had been preempted by the colonisers. Barron Field wrote off Australia as 'prose-dull', and hoped that the wings of poesy—as he fatuously put it—would soon whirl him away to a more amenable clime. His charge, having become formulaic, was repeated by Stephen Spender in 1954 during a world tour sponsored by the Congress for Cultural Freedom (a shady organisation bankrolled by the CIA). Spender travelled first to Paris, Rome and Athens, then at last touched down in Darwin. Only a fool or an arrogant ninny would have expected Darwin to be other than anti-climactic after three capitals that are cornerstones of European civilisation. Spender, however, thought it worth reflecting on the disparity in his journal: 'The countries of prose and the countries of poetry: this contrast struck me the moment I arrived.' A revelation! Inartistic in itself, Australia was even declared to be an unfit home for art made elsewhere. In 1955 at the National Gallery in London, the actor John Gielgud spotted 'a lovely Tiepolo of the Banquet of Cleopatra lent by the Melbourne Art Gallery'. Sounding, at least on paper, like an outraged Wildean dowager, he asked, 'How on earth did it ever get there?'

There was no question of Australians being permitted to create art of their own. The language we spoke was disqualified, being no more than a crude, unlettered adulteration of the mother tongue. Louis, one of the six precious soliloquists in Virginia Woolf's novel *The Waves*, is mortified because—as he keeps on dolefully repeating—his father is 'a banker in Brisbane'. Sent back to England to be schooled, he is teased in the playground and flushes to discover that he has an Australian accent. That instantly puts paid to his ambition to become a poet. After all, the English believed that Australian birds could not sing, just as they insisted that our flowers had no scent; would-be Australian writers shared this disablement. I remember my distress when, not much older than Louis, I first read this book during my schooldays in Tasmania. This ignorant, snobbish writer had sentenced me to muteness. Well, in time I recovered my voice (and I'm currently using it to settle some scores). Elsewhere in *The Waves*, Woolf describes Piccadilly Circus underground station as the centre of the universe, civilisation's hub. Nowadays, I avoid the raucous, rancid, herded squalor of Piccadilly, and smirk as I recall Virginia Woolf's view of it as the earth's navel. Louis, however, never raises his voice in protest. Instead he makes himself useful to the commercial empire controlled by London: he works for a shipping firm in the City, and sends vessels 'to the remotest parts of the globe; replete with lavatories and gymnasiums'. That is his way of overcoming his unfortunate birth on the periphery. But he accepts the grim prohibition imposed by English culture, and writes no poems.

Woolf merely pitied poor Australia. Norman Douglas, a Scottish litterateur who moved to Capri early in the twentieth century, decried the very idea of the place in a fit of exasperation so dyspeptic that Rex Ingamells quoted it in his Jindyworobak manifesto in 1938, just to make clear what we were up against.

Douglas was provoked by the intrusion of eucalypts, planted around his beloved Mediterranean in the mistaken hope that they might prevent malaria. He accused the trees of 'manifold iniquities', including a 'diabolical thirst' and a 'demoralising aspect'. He diagnosed 'precocious senility and vice', thought their peeling bark was a symptom of some 'unmentionable skin disease', and castigated their foliage for its 'perverse, anti-human' denial of shade. Douglas assumed that such freaks suited their own blasted heath. He had once looked, he said, at a book called *Dead Heart of Australia*: the illustrations 'gave me a nightmare from which I shall never recover'. In this reckoning, Australia remained the world's eternal and irredeemable underside, a penal colony to which you were transported in your own worst dreams.

The 'dead heart' was never more than a figure of speech, but such figurations can themselves be deadly. The heart of the country was not dead at all, but buzzing, throbbing, seething with life. Perhaps that gave the colonisers an incentive to kill it. During the 1950s, British scientists tested atomic bombs in the outback: Australia with its nullified terrain served as a convenient laboratory for experimenting with annihilation. In 1993 the Japanese acolytes of the cult known as Aum Supreme Truth rehearsed another, stealthier apocalypse in Western Australia. The guru Shoko Asahara and his specialist in bioweaponry entered the country on tourist visas, though they brought along in their baggage a small armoury of mining gear and stocks of acids and toxins. They acquired a sheep station on the edge of the Gibson Desert, supposedly to be used as a place of 'healing and worship'. Here they undevoutly fossicked for uranium and also synthesised sarin nerve gas, which they tried out on a flock of merinos. Their next experimental animals were the commuting sheep on the Tokyo subway. Prophets come out of the deserts, as AD Hope said. But who goes into those deserts? Saviours on suicide missions like Patrick White's Voss, nihilists, and rational fanatics who believe that the correct formula in chemistry or physics can uncreate our world.

Given the rhetorical arsenals trained on us, we are lucky to have survived. Unlike the Americans, we fought no war with Britain, and have no revolutionary myth to enshrine our independence. The convicts failed to tip Governor Phillip's tea into Sydney Harbour. A rebellious flag emblazoned with the Southern Cross was raised above the Eureka Stockade, but it later entered into a neutered alliance with the Union Jack. We still have a head of state who resides in the other hemisphere and pays courtesy calls on us every few years. But culturally, the process of liberation is just about complete—and perhaps my generation should feel selfishly grateful for the delay, because we have had the chance to live through Australia's recreation of itself.

Artists now know how to look at and listen to the country, so at last the eucalypts have had justice done to them. When Fred Williams came home from England in 1956, he was startled to find a landscape that looked 'unstructured ... with no centre of interest'. The perception pointed him towards a new way of painting Australia's free, random, endlessly exfoliating space. Williams's singed trees after a bushfire don't mind looking scraggy, and they flaunt a 'system of radication' that Norman Douglas ridiculed: they seem to be suspended in the brown air, not fastened to the soil. Life surges through their gaunt trunks, and the very flecks of paint are seeds, disseminating energy across a country that has been renewed by its close brush with death.

In one of his poems, Les Murray compares a Japanese plum tree with a flowering gum, and decides that the petals shed by the import give it no advantage. True, it makes an 'exquisitely precious/ artistic bloom', but 'unpetalled gum-debris' is even more astonishing, because that litter rears up in

> a tower of fabulous swish tatters,
> a map hoisted upright, a crusted
> riverbed with up-country show towns.

Swishing and showy fabulousness are qualities you associate with models on catwalks, whose dress is expensive even if tattered; the way Murray looks at it, the tree has a beauty that is gaudy, riotous, as exuberant as the sneezing fits that its blossoms provoke. In his novel *Eucalyptus*, Murray Bail sets out to differentiate the varieties of gum and to tell the stories associated with them, making them as idiosyncratic as if they were literary characters. At the end, Bail's hero sits on a verandah and takes stock of 'the many different species of trees, described by their different names'. 'A forest,' he concludes, 'is a language.' The phrase reminds me of those poles outside the Museum of Sydney, which—if you get near enough—turn out to have recorded voices in them, invisible spirits that describe and commemorate the first settlement. The idea that eucalypts might be eloquent would have horrified Norman Douglas. For him, the only noise the ghastly things could make was a metallic rustling like 'the sibilant chatterings of ghosts'. But Bail's loquacious trees become articulate because he knows how to translate their tall stories.

With an equal ambition, Peter Sculthorpe sets the country's silent, apparently moribund heart to music in his symphonic poem *The Fifth Continent*. In doing so he cunningly disarms one of those colonising tourists who made such peremptory, premature judgements about Australia. Sculthorpe's meditation on the landscape uses extracts from DH Lawrence's political novel *Kangaroo*, written after he spent all of ten weeks here in 1924. Lawrence's summary of the country was characteristically deadly: he called it 'humanly non-existent'. Did he, like the snarling Robert Mitchum, think that no human beings lived here? He specified that it could be seen but not heard, like a cowed Victorian infant: the 'vast continent' was 'really void of speech'. The personified Kangaroo in his book is not much less monstrous than Barron Field's hippogriff. Lawrence's hero is a lawyer with a marsupial nickname, who leads a secret fascist movement; he's the demagogic embodiment of the vulgar, totalitarian Ocker mob.

When Sculthorpe chose extracts from the novel to be spoken between the movements of *The Fifth Continent*, he edited out the illiberal politics. But he kept the nagging critique of the bush. The trees, Lawrence says over and over again, are hoary, ghostly, phantom-like. The uninhabited land looks 'lost'—though all he means is that his narrator, Lawrence's own alias, is lost in it and longs 'for Europe with hungry longing'.

These accusing words are neutralised by the music. While Lawrence complains of deracination, Sculthorpe's orchestra puts down roots as we listen. *The Fifth Continent* begins in outer space, as a faint, chilly music of the spheres illustrates the narrator's claim that a trip to Australia is a voyage to another planet. An audible shock marks his crash landing on the surface of this alien world. He expects 'young Australia' to outlast the decay of the northern hemisphere; as he says so, a thumping call to attention on the drums warns of Sculthorpe's personal, patriotic agenda. Then comes the section that Sculthorpe calls 'Outback', which contains Lawrence's attack on the gruesome gum trees. Lawrence never got to the actual outback, and based his omniscient over-view of Australia on glimpses of Perth, Sydney, and a mining town on the south coast of New South Wales. Though the words nervously cling to the urbanised edge of the continent, Sculthorpe's music speaks from the interior. Under the narrator's complaint we hear the *didgeridoo*, which supplies a grounding. It as if the scorched land were droning in a register far beneath the sweetly pining violins. And in the section on the Pacific, the keening of taped winds allows Australian nature itself to vocalise.

Lawrence's narrative records the impressions of a British traveller. Appropriating it, Sculthorpe gives it an Australian accent. I remember listening on the radio to the first performance of *The Fifth Continent* in 1963, broadcast live from the City Hall in Hobart. The speaker then was James McAuley; when the Tasmanian Symphony Orchestra recorded the work a few years ago, Sculthorpe himself spoke the narration. At the end of *Kangaroo*, the dissatisfied Lawrentian pilgrim sails off to San Francisco and prepares to denounce another dead, empty continent. But in Sculthorpe's epilogue, the narrator makes no mention of departure. He is not just visiting; born here, he intends to stay. He sits by the shore as the strings evoke a mystical, sunstruck bliss. It was in such a place that the composer Percy Grainger dreamed up the idea of a music freed from European strictures: the possibility of tonal freedom came to him, as he said in 1938, while he studied the movement of waves on Brighton Beach in Melbourne. Soothed, calmed, Sculthorpe finally quietens the European instruments, and gives the last word to the didgeridoo. It echoes from some remote distance in space and time, and what it chants is the song of the Australian earth.

three
Down Under

The Australia I grew up in during the 1950s was as white as starch, and about as stiff. Everyone adhered to Anglo-Saxondom, even if their lineage was doubtful. During the war, my father's family re-spelled its name to eliminate a treasonous Teutonic K, and there was general embarrassment when my grandmother, during the last months of her life, reverted to babbling in Swedish. My mother's people were called Smith, which could not have been more respectable—except that, in the rural valley she came from, Smith was also one of the code names adopted by descendants of the Tasmanian Aborigines, officially extinct but discreetly thriving on the margins of society.

We huddled in a mock-up of suburban England, remorselessly bright and bland. Spatial paranoia made us thankful for our isolation from the rest of the world. Back then, Europe was a scrabble board of unlucky countries—the source of wars and of food that tasted too spicy, inhabited by people whose languages were funny and who, in taciturn Australia, gesticulated when they spoke. These infidels were rare enough to seem peculiar. I recall just three from those days: a Greek fishmonger (foreigners were always aromatic), a Polish labourer who worked with my father and patiently bore his teasing, and a dour Dutch newsagent around the corner. It wasn't until I got to university that I made the acquaintance of a Latvian family whose name contained a z, as heady and fetching as a zither or a gipsy's violin. Before I ate with my friends the Rozensteins, I didn't know that bread came in any shade but white.

New Australians were treated with wary raillery. While on probation, they had to learn the appropriate oaths, shout their rounds, barrack for one of the local footy teams. Only then might they be accepted. It didn't occur to us to wonder what they thought of us, which might have been a mercy. The photographer Helmut Newton, born to a Jewish family in Berlin, left Germany in 1938 and shipped out to Singapore. Interned there, he was sent on to Australia in 1940. He was undelighted by the prospect. 'Nobody ever thought of Australia,' he spluttered in his autobiography, 'I mean, whoever thought of Australia? Nobody thought of Australia. You didn't go to Australia!' That about says it, after he has excoriated the country by naming it four times. On arrival, Newton was categorised as an enemy alien and sent to an internment camp at Tatura near Shepparton, Victoria—preferable to Auschwitz, I'd have thought. There were few escape attempts, because, as Newton noted, there was nothing to escape to. Eventually released, he travelled into Melbourne, walked out of the railway station, and burst into tears. His sobbing fit did not express gratitude to his new home. What provoked it was revulsion: 'I'd never seen anything quite as ugly as Flinders Street.' Newton even refused to give Australia any credit for his rampant sexual success. He took up with a girl who, as well as carnal favours, supplied him with rationed beer and contraband Craven As. Yet he couldn't pardon her vulgarity, and corrected the grammatical errors she made while she egged him on in bed. Despite our unworthiness, I suppose Newton found his Australian passport convenient.

There's a similar case history in Patrick White's *The Burnt Ones*, though the outcome is different. A blithe Sydney market researcher learns about desire from a squat, peppery Hungarian immigrant. Her demon lover considers Australian girls to be 'visout Temperament', and decries the soullessness of a country that consists of only 'stike and bodies'. Unlike Newton's grammatically slipshod girlfriend, she responds to his criticism by flogging him with a grazier's stockwhip: an apt initiatic rite for a New Australian, you might think. 'Are you ze Defel perhaps?' he asks, sore but satiated.

White relied on a diabolism like this to induce a fall in the sunny paradise of Australia. Vice, including the deviancy of art, was the prerogative of the elderly, wily north, and in White's novels it ravages a southern society that is only virtuous because it lacks imagination. He devoted much of his life to an assault on the country's cowering conventionality. In 1958 he wrote a letter to some friends in England, declaring 'How sick I am of the bloody word AUSTRALIA'. He capitalised the offending noun, as if it were a graphic shout. Though he envied their expatriation, he had to stay at home—he explained—so he could fling 'about six or seven more of my Australian novels' in the faces of his countrymen. But he was not convinced that this would make any difference to characters like Mrs Golson in *The Twyborn Affair*, who is the offspring of a manufacturer of sweat-free felt hats for Sydneysiders. Spending her sweat-free money on a trip overseas, she recoils from a revelation of decadent sexual mischief in the south of France, and rushes back to her comfortingly ordinary hubby: as White puts it with a sneer, 'she fled towards Curly, honesty, *Australia*'. This time the country's name is italicised for reassurance.

To overcome what he called 'the Australian emptiness', White imported a succession of visionary fanatics, addled mystics and sexual mutants, who could not be grown on native ground: the German explorer Voss, the martyred Jewish refugee Himmelfarb in *Riders in the Chariot*, and the defrocked Byzantine empress impersonated by the androgynous Eddie in *The Twyborn Affair*. These were his antidote to the poor Britons brought out on assisted passages after the war, who recreated their drab Midlands in the tropics. Like magi who carry bad news, White's characters smuggled tragedy and madness in their luggage. In *The Solid Mandala*, Waldo—one of these ecstatic maniacs—proposes to the daughter of the Feinsteins. She listens to his lyrical babbling, then refuses him. 'They were in Australia again', White comments: it is a bumping de-levitation, a lapse from poetry to prose. Eddie or Eadith, commuting between hemispheres and genders in *The Twyborn Affair*, understands the sacrifice that will be necessary when he repatriates himself. He therefore exchanges his spangled 'European drag' for the moleskins and elastic-sided boots of a jackeroo.

White began to think about *Voss* while he was living in London during the blitz. As the German bombs fell around his Pimlico bedsitter, their violence merged with his own vengeful, disruptive creativity: 'A seed was sown in what had the appearance of barren ground,' he remembered. A book can detonate like a grenade. In *The Twyborn Affair*, a scandalous rumour circulates in the prim Sydney of the 1920s. It is reported that a cockie's wife is reading Proust down in the Riverina. However will the cockie keep her down on the farm, now that she has read about the perversity of Paree? The same antipodal vision persists in the stories collected by David Malouf under the title of *Antipodes*. Malouf's immigrant characters are less Messiah-like than White's; sad and secretive, they retain perturbing memories of their 'previous world'. White's eccentrics find a similarity between Europe's abraded history and their own hard-bitten land. Visiting Greece in *The Aunt's Story*, Theodora Goodman recognises its suffering austerity and says, 'I too come from a country of bones'. Malouf's people lack this appetite for agony, though they do subversively hunger for rye bread and Sacher torte. They are glad to have escaped from tragic Europe, and hope that in Australia they can live it down. But it haunts them: it is their 'dark side', perilously enticing. A Polish refugee, comfortably re-established on Sydney's North Shore, returns to Europe and shudders at the 'dark, death-obsessed' culture of a Mediterranean island where gunmen stage a coup. Another Australian pilgrim exchanges his native sun for the misty, morbid city of Bruges, whose stagnant canals and deserted churches exude a 'high worship of death'.

What Malouf has noticed is an itchy, dissatisfied national trait. Rather than congratulating ourselves on our reprieve from the abysmal past, we demand some share in the other hemisphere's remote history of conflict. Hence Malouf's recent lecture paying homage to the commemoration of Anzac Day, which he admires because it brings home to us a 'sense of the tragic'. A society that does not ponder the mystery of death and devise rituals to play-act its onset—dawn marches, trumpet reveilles—is, Malouf argues, 'a poor one'. It's an inimitably Australian notion, not at all universal in its relevance. The United States, for instance, has officially outlawed death; its religion is a man-made immortality, a cult of surgically-assisted eternal youth. Other countries get along without our thanatological gloom, but Australia certainly envies the northern hemisphere its tragedies. Some writers even argue that those catastrophes have been restaged here. Peter Carey likens the Australian penal colony of the eighteenth and nineteenth centuries to Auschwitz, and Robert Hughes sees the same regime as a precursor of Stalin's gulag. I admire the brawny bravado of the pretence, but I'm not convinced.

By common consent, our harsh beginnings were soon forgotten. Tragedy arrived later, as the bequest of European malcontents like those in Patrick White's novels. For White, modernism was a licensed sadism, and he saw himself as Australia's self-appointed scourge, destined to hurt the country into modernity. While writing *The Vivisector*, about a painter who conducts wrenching experiments on the visible world, he reflected that 'writers are charged with "cruelty" more often painters', though he was sure that Picasso and Dubuffet merited the accusation. For him, cruelty was a legitimate and necessary procedure, almost a profession of faith, and European artists showed him how to excruciate a tame local reality. He called *The Aunt's Story* 'a kind of Klee', because Theo's insanity—an ailment she contracts in the degenerating Europe of the late 1930s—turns her into one of the jittery stick figures drawn by Paul Klee. Preparing to write about the death of Voss, he played a record of Bartók's violin concerto: its etherised, evaporating sounds dictated what his words should do.

It was music, infiltrating the southern hemisphere like those radioactive winds in *On the Beach*, that brought to Australia the European drama of sensual torment and existential strife. Gwen Harwood wrote a series of poems about Professor Dietrich Kröte, a missionary for this morbid cult. Kröte is a maudlin alcoholic beached in Brisbane, teaching the piano to suburban brats while he tries to find 'what more the city held than brick and stone'. Back in Europe, his own teacher was taught by Liszt, but this lineage means nothing to the pretentious hostesses at whose afternoon receptions he plays sugary waltzes or the mourners who hire him to make an electronic organ wheeze at the crematorium. The unhappy Kröte frowns like his plaster bust of Beethoven; sick in hospital, he at least has the chance to indulge in a crazed cadenza of fury, and he rages 'fortissimo in German'. No wonder Mrs Humphries thought that little Barry's fondness for Wagner and Strauss was unnecessary (as Dame Edna would say) and probably unpatriotic. 'Must you play all that continental music?' she used to ask. 'It wasn't all that long ago we were at war with those people.' My parents also flinched when I put on my scratchy gramophone records of German symphonies, and prepared for complaints from the neighbours. What good had it done to change the K in our surname? Kröte, a synonym for Kraut, begins with the same incriminating letter.

Music's value lay in its sedition, its challenge to our tight-lipped, temperate society. As Moraïtis plays a cello concerto in *The Aunt's Story*, Theo hears 'one long barely subjugated cry': an outpouring of grief disallowed in laconic, stoical Australia, where battlers were expected to struggle on without whingeing. Mrs Feinstein in *The Solid Mandala* has this European music in her voice, though she tries to keep it 'light, giggly, and Australian'; despite her repressive efforts, the rich ripe cello notes of opulent melancholy keep making themselves heard. In one of Malouf's stories, a Viennese matron transplanted to Elizabeth Bay in Sydney goes to an orchestral concert at the Opera House, and allows the music to express a misery to which she can't give utterance: 'Terrible Tchaikovsky bloomed all over the hall'.

A Greek woman in *The Aunt's Story* asks Theo whether she has ever seen a burning piano. The surreal image sums up the combustible excitement of art, which ignites or incinerates the artist. But the searing ardour of music was sometimes deflated by the worldly, practical local musicians who performed it. In 1977 Patrick White met Joan Sutherland, after seeing her as the suicidal nun in Puccini's *Suor Angelica*. Sutherland gobbled her supper, told White—with a full mouth, he noted—that she'd never read any of his books, made matters worse by praising Colleen McCullough, and in general behaved as if she would rather have been outside kicking a football. Her Ocker demeanour reminded White that he was still in Australia, where operatic conduct was not permitted.

Malouf, in a story about a soprano whose repertoire overlaps with Sutherland's, gives a more sympathetic account of the paradox. His heroine Alicia Vale, like Sutherland, sings Lucia di Lammermoor, Lucrezia Borgia, Semiramide and Adriana Lecouvreur. Careers devoted to such works involve a traversal of realms as insubstantial as fluttering stage sets: Babylon, Venice, the foggy Scottish Highlands. But after conquering the world, the tough 'colonial girls' listed by Malouf—'the Alicias, the

Melbas, the Marjories, the Joans'—'come home to die in the suburbs'. For Malouf, the coexistence of sublimity and crudity, the juggling of stratospheric Europe and pedestrian Australia, only adds to the diva's mystery. Because White thought of his own repatriation as a living death, suffered only for art's sake, this return to the suburbs seemed to him to be a betrayal. Australia demystifies the diva, and Sutherland irritated White because she apparently enjoyed reverting to ordinariness. She further complicated matters at her farewell performance of *Les Huguenots* in Sydney in 1990. To end the evening, she touchingly warbled 'Home Sweet Home', after which she flew back to her chalet in tax-free Switzerland. She was not, it seemed, intending to expire in Woollahra. But there was an epilogue. In 1994 she shed the last dignified trappings of diva-dom and returned to Australia to play the fly-blown matriarch in the film of Steele Rudd's *On Our Selection*. From Babylon's hanging gardens to the parched Darling Downs; from Rossini's murderous, incestuous Semiramide to Steele Rudd's Ma, who gropes under the hens to see if they've laid, cooks parrot stew for her famished brood, and feeds scraps to the pigs—this was exactly the plummeting fall between hemispheres that alarmed White.

He expected musicians to be exponents of anguish. Brought out on concert tours by the ABC, they were ambassadors for delicious suffering and uplifting catharsis. You could expatriate yourself by listening to the sounds they produced. But some of these musicians put down roots that went deeper into native soil than those of British settlers, who often thought of life in Australia as a camp temporarily pitched in the wilderness. Once in the United States, I bought a battered copy of a book about Arnhem Land, with the previous owner's name written on the flyleaf—'Claudio Arrau, Perth 1957'. Arrau was a virtuoso pianist born in Chile, who became fascinated by Aboriginal culture during his concert tours here. He was not the first such convert. Richard Goldner, who founded Musica Viva, was a Romanian violinist trained in Vienna; arriving in Australia as a refugee, he formed the Monomeeth String Quartet, which took its name from an Aboriginal word for peace and harmony. In 1940 the Orphic spell of music could hardly express itself in German, so it adopted a local idiom.

The Czech choreographer Edouard Borovansky was touring Australia when the Nazis occupied the Sudetenland in 1938. He stayed put, recruited his own company, and in 1940 staged a ballet called *Vltava*, using Smetana's tone-poem about the legendary river that flows through Czechoslovakia. But Australia was a dry terrain, lacking mermaids; in 1946 Borovansky dramatised its spiritual travails in the ballet *Terra Australis*, with a blacked-up lover in tribal body paint fighting a white conquistador for possession of the country. Australia was represented on stage by the stark white trunk of a dead tree, holding a tortured balletic pose. It sounds like Stravinsky's *Rite of Spring* transferred from Russia to the outback. European modernists yearned for primal worlds, alternatives to the dreary industrial nineteenth century.

Tales of Two Hemispheres

Picasso collected African masks, Eisenstein filmed the bloodthirsty gods sculpted by the Aztecs. Borovansky and his fellow émigré artists—whose achievements were documented in *The Europeans*, a touring exhibition mounted by the National Gallery of Australia in 1997—peeled away the thin, insulated coating of colonialism and disclosed the same primordial gulfs in Australia.

They began by looking at the ground and making use of what they found there. Locked up as an enemy alien, the surrealist Klaus Friedeberger pieced together assemblages from the flotsam and jetsam he scavenged around the camp: scraps of asbestos, bones, barbed wire, wooden spars—the unkempt ingredients of vernacular Australia. Claudio Alcorso, held at Hay in western New South Wales, remembered his fellow internees using firewood to carve utensils, after which they graduated to non-utilitarian sculptures. A gang sent out to fell trees along the Murray River tested the consistency of wet clay on the bank and brought back samples to be shaped and fired in a kiln. 'All sorts of pots and forms were made,' Alcorso reported. His Latin connoisseurship of the soil prepared Alcorso for his later career as a wine-grower. In 1947 he moved his textile factory to Tasmania, where he also defied the Barossa Valley's monopoly by establishing a vineyard. His friends shook their heads sceptically, but Alcorso consulted a European precedent that went back two thousand years to 'when viticulture expanded from the hot, traditional regions of Greece and southern Italy, to Gallia and to the Rhine'. If you invert the map, reversing south and north,

South Australia is Greece or Spain—best, scoffed Alcorso, for producing sweet sherries—whereas Tasmania corresponds to France or Germany. He therefore planted some cuttings of Rhine riesling grapes, and contentedly watched them flourish.

On his headland in the Derwent, Alcorso constructed a Roman villa from Coles Bay red granite, King Billy pine and limed Tasmanian oak. But he knew that there was an Aboriginal midden on the site, full of culinary implements used by 'the old people' and mussel shells they had discarded. He was careful to honour his predecessors, and paid tribute to their 'tutelary gods'. Nor did he clear the casuarinas along the river bank, as the intolerant first settlers might have done. The affinity between Mediterranean paganism and Aboriginal veneration of the earth seemed natural; reliance on Anglo-Saxon modes of behaviour and belief could only cause disorientation and bewilderment.

New Australians like Alcorso renovated Australian life. They despised the boiled potatoes dished up at every meal, and the compulsory mugs of milky tea; Italian market gardeners grew tomatoes and basil, and in the cities other Italians opened espresso bars. Culture starts in the soil and feels its way upwards. Herbs, vegetables and coffee beans pointed eventually towards Italy's most glorious and grandiose export, so Alcorso became the chairman of the Australian Opera. As a manufacturer of textiles, he also persuaded Australian housewives to stop dressing as if they were still in the Home Counties, and hired artists to replace the insipid floral prints that hung in everyone's wardrobe. Donald Friend's silk-screen motifs represented pearl divers in the Torres Strait, Margaret Preston used shapes from bark painting, William Constable sketched a corroboree, and a scarf by Roy Dalgarno evoked Arnhem Land. Why should women want to impersonate roses or merge with imaginary hedgerows? The Viennese milliner Stella Fraenkel came to Sydney after Hitler annexed Austria, leaving behind clients like Marlene Dietrich. She too dared her Australian customers to be more exotic. After a trip to hunt crocodiles in New Guinea, she was reported to be designing feathered headdresses copied from the regalia of warriors she had spotted in the highlands.

In 1929 the French surrealists published a world map, on which they either shrunk countries or inflated them according to their surrealistic content. New Guinea, whose savagery had been extolled by the painter Emil Nolde, stretched across the ocean all the way from the New Hebrides to Borneo, looking more than ever like a pterodactyl with open jaws. New Zealand also swelled in size and significance: it boasted geysers and cannibals, both of which were considered surreal. But the Australian continent came out looking as small as Tasmania (which was omitted altogether). Such dismissals were easy to get away with in those days, when DH Lawrence declared us to be humanly null and void.

A few years later, a European artist who had actually seen the country made another map of it, catching its planetary strangeness and its gaunt beauty. The designer Gert Sellheim was born in Estonia, studied architecture in Germany, and came to Australia as a young man in 1926. His diploma was not recognised, so he worked as a wharfie in Fremantle—a typical initiation for an over-qualified New Australian. In 1930 Sellheim established himself in Melbourne and began to produce travel posters. After a wartime spell behind barbed wire at Tatura, he was commissioned to design a corporate logo for Qantas: he conceived the flying red kangaroo (which at first had wings that made it look like a scary, volatile Jurassic reptile). Sellheim was one of those migrants who looked beyond prim, anaemic Anglo-Saxon Australia to the ancient land mass of Gondwana, which broke up as it drifted across the ocean and left us with our stranded population of marsupials. He decorated his Christmas cards with totemic animals copied from Aboriginal rock galleries, not sheep and oxen kneeling in prayer around a manger.

In 1937 Sellheim designed a map for a book commemorating the 150th anniversary of colonial settlement. The result was anything but a celebration of British occupancy. On a double-page spread, the continent floats off centre and is also tilted at an angle. Long after its secession from Gondwana, it is still not yet securely fixed in place. Never has it looked more like a life-raft, which is how the European immigrants and exiles must have thought of it when they scrambled aboard, saved from the wreckage of their own continent. A play of chiaroscuro crosses it, following the track of the sun through its time zones. Cape York flares like a candle, and the east coast glows; the land darkens as your eye moves west. The shading is a reminder of Australia's enormity, since even the sun can't see it all at once. It hints as well at the spiritual combat going on within that vast space. A marginal inscription on the map notes that Captain Cook first sighted the south-eastern corner, where settlement began. But Sellheim traces a galleon in full sail—drawn in white ink like a ghost ship—on the west coast, which is where he made his own landfall at Fremantle; from its rigging to its low, heavy stern, this phantasmal vessel stretches from the top of Western Australia almost to the bottom, and its prow breaches the land like an amphibious invader. A pole like a cannon points out from the deck, aiming across the desert towards the north-eastern tip.

It is here, in the section where the land is brightest, that Sellheim has gathered a collection of creatures imitated, like those on his Christmas cards, from Aboriginal rock art. A kangaroo bounds across the Northern Territory, and a crocodile swims towards the elongated tip of Queensland. On the coast are four human figures, corroboree dancers who might be raising their hands in fear or surrender, aware of the menace announced by that outsize British ship. Along the Great Barrier Reef, Sellheim places the white imprints of a turtle and a platypus: emigrants paddling off in search of another safe haven, now that their native land has been taken from them. The inscription at the base of the map sums up the approved version of events in self-important capital letters: 'AND THUS THE WORLD'S OLDEST CONTINENT WAS OPENED TO CIVILISATION'. The testimony of Sellheim's image suggests other possibilities. It's not true that the world's oldest continent was merely an area of darkness that submissively awaited enlightenment. Nor did it need to be 'opened to civilisation', penetrated by force. And what kind of civilisation needs a gunboat as its emissary?

Meanwhile, high on the east coast in Sellheim's map, the terrorised dancers and their panicked animals prepare their evacuation. Revving up on its bouncy tail, the flying kangaroo is poised to hop across oceans. The next tales I'll tell are about what happened when Australians, unloaded from fleets of Qantas roos, inspected that so-called civilisation on its home ground.

four
Up Over

Looking back, I wonder—blushing a bit—if I entered London for the first time on bended knees. It was the summer of 1968; I had been on an ocean liner for a month, cooped in a throbbing closet that had no porthole because it was way below the waterline. After landing in Southampton, I took a train up from the south coast and walked across Waterloo Bridge into a world whose towers and spires and domes were made, for me, of words not bricks. I soon had my first experience of being absorbed in and effaced by a crowd of strangers who could not have cared less about my existence. But nothing could diminish my dazed exhilaration. Despite the heat, cold shocks of excitement jolted through me. I should have crawled across the bridge, to complete my exhausting trek between hemispheres and ages.

Attitudes, mercifully, have changed since then, and so have methods of transport. My protracted voyage across two oceans counted as a quest. While the boat dug its way through the waves as if arduously ploughing them, I waited, dreamed, and hoped I'd be worthy. Today you are catapulted between hemispheres during one long night on a jet of hot air. If you're lucky you spend most of the journey in a coma (or watching videos, which is the next best thing). Arrival is a downer. Heathrow before dawn, with its bleary neon and sallow shuffling masses, makes you wonder why you bothered. There is no bright bridge to walk across into London. Instead you spend an hour in a fetid railway tunnel, or even longer in a fuming traffic jam.

The Australian response, quite properly, is to begin complaining. Patrick White, having landed at Heathrow in 1976, groused about the lack of trolleys and porters—although Sidney Nolan was waiting for him once he got through customs, and presumably helped with the luggage. When Murray Bail landed at Heathrow a few years earlier, he took the double-decker bus to the old airline terminal at Victoria, and felt himself 'swallowed by the flat maze' of 'grime and slate', conducted into the city through 'narrow passageways'. The hero of White's early novel *The Living and the Dead* has a similar experience when he emerges from Victoria Station. He is submerged by commonplaceness; personal identity is erased, and he must 'swim in the confused sea that was anybody's London'. Bail, on the bus's upper deck, took care to feel 'above it all'. Resisting absorption, he reminded himself that he was not British. Better this defiance than my prostration. I've come to cherish the hard-headed practicality of the hero's wife in Henry Handel Richardson's *The Fortunes of Richard*

Mahony. She is English, and has been dragged back to London by her self-improving colonial husband. Richard, who revels in the city's museums and art galleries, contrasts England's congested history with the empty geography of Australia. Mary accompanies him on his cultural rounds, but pines for her adopted country: 'Privately she thought London not a patch on Ballarat'.

When Bail got off the airport bus and started to haul his suitcases, he assumed a stony face to cover his vulnerability. That truculence catches the mood of the Australian abroad, in those days at least. Sent to the bottom of the earth, we spent weeks on the water toiling back up to what we thought of as the top. Having invested our fondest hopes in that remote goal, we risked a wounding disillusionment. At least the sun shone for me as I advanced across Waterloo Bridge. When Melba reached London in 1886, she shuddered at its grey skies, dirty wharves and soiled chimneys. 'How can I sing in such gloom?' she asked, as if she were a nightingale that had migrated to the wrong continent. She tried out a trill to cheer herself up: the opening salvo in her campaign to vanquish what she called—in the farewell letter she wrote to her compatriots in 1924—'the big world outside'.

Melba's initial trill possessed the ballistic force of a cannonade. The rest of us, taking stock of our new surroundings, were less sure that we would survive. Many trials of strength awaited us, beginning with the weather. Your first northern winter tests your fortitude: having grown up in Hobart, I was at least prepared for chillblains and snow flurries. During the 1950s Christopher Koch—ravaged by hunger pangs in a Notting Hill bedsit as he hoarded coins for the gas meter—roused himself to confront the 'iron, majestic cold' with its 'sheer, icy edge'. He knew he was engaged in an elemental fight. In Helen Hodgman's *Blue Skies*, the narrator has a brother who—like Koch, like Hodgman, like me—absconds from Tasmania to England. Settled in a bleak Midlands town, he paints a tropical landscape on the blind wall behind his terraced house, then decamps to London and leaves his wife and child to face 'the snow and ice and the miserable solitude'. The north was a frigid inferno; it had the power to destroy you.

No doubt we exaggerated the risks, probably because we had a dim recollection of what happened to the first Australian tourists. Recruiting posters for the 1914–18 war deceptively advertised the army as a chance to see the world, hoping to sign up immigrants who wanted a cheap trip back to Europe. My generation parodied such propaganda in the banners with which we protested against the Vietnam War: 'Join the Army! Travel to exotic and distant lands. Meet exciting, unusual people—and kill them.' Or, as at Gallipoli, be killed by them.

Australia's disenchantment with the wider world began when the diggers were given a few days' leave from the trenches and allowed to look around. Leonard Mann, wounded at Passchendaele in 1917, published a novel about the war in 1932. In *Flesh in Armour* he describes some infantrymen who squat on the railings in Trafalgar Square and survey the city. The Strand is a showcase for colonial wares: each of the Australian states has offices, with shop windows exhibiting native fauna and farm produce. I recall the same proud display half a century later. If you read the map like a loyalist, the axis that held the hemispheres together still ran from the Aldwych along the Strand and into the Mall—and as it happened, this was my first walk in London, after I left the bridge. You started at Australia House with its piles of hometown newspapers and ended at the gates of Buckingham Palace, where you looked up to see if the flag was flying. On the way between one and the other, reprising your journey of ten thousand miles, you could stop off to buy Vegemite at a shop in a side street that ran down to the Embankment. The premises that belonged to the state governments were long ago sold off, and they now tout burgers, lattes and mobile phones. Despite my regrets, it's good to be reminded that not everyone trudged that route as deferentially as I did in 1968. One of the diggers in Leonard Mann's novel remembers how grandly Collins Street ascends its hill, flanked by elms and plane trees, and sneers at the drabness of the Strand. Even Admiral Nelson, who looks 'small and disproportionate … in the dirty mist', is dragged down from his column. Has he been ordered to stand up there in disgrace, as penance for dallying with Lady Hamilton and asking Hardy to kiss him? This 'cold alien England', for which the colonial soldiers are expected to die, startles them into an understanding of their 'distinctive Australian nationality'.

Up Over

David Malouf has often written about the mental confusion of such men, expelled from their safe, familiar lives in Australia by foreign wars. In *Fly Away Peter*, a young birdwatcher named Jim leaves his sanctuary on the Queensland coast and goes off to fight and die at Armentières in 1914. The novel finds a sad, touching disparity between the migrations of birds and the forced marches of uprooted men. Jim marvels at the birds, whose tiny brains can englobe the entire world, guiding them to and fro between Europe and Australia. They come to rest in this refuge for a season, but they are not refugees: that term has a human and political reference, evoking the arbitrary flight of displaced persons aiming leaky boats at the Australian coast. Men, taking part in 'big migrations' of their own on troop ships, lack the avian capacity to balance the hemispheres, and many of them do not complete the round trip.

Malouf worries about the zeal of the volunteers, who believe that in joining the army they have 'finally come into the real world at last'. As Australians so often used to do, they assume their own world to be unreal, or less than real: Melba's 'big world' implies that our world is small. A later Malouf novel about another war evokes the 'great world', beside which our remote, placid world at home looks insignificant—even though that 'great world' is actually no more than a disused theme park in Thailand, where some POWs camp while slaving on the railway. Jim in *Fly Away Peter* thinks that he will graduate into reality when he puts on his uniform. Instead he enters the surreal nightmare of the seeping, stinking trenches on the Western Front, where he keeps company with rats not birds.

The rodents feast on decay; they are 'familiars of death, creatures of the underworld'. But their burrowing and scavenging remind Jim that he too is a digger. Birds cruise round the curve of the planet during their annual flights between hemispheres. Men, terrestrial not aerial, can only make themselves at home by digging graves for themselves. As he dies, Jim begins an imaginary dig. He thinks he sees hundreds of his fellow corpses bent over clawing at the black mucky soil; they are on their way home, 'digging through to the other side', taking 'the direct route—straight through'. Creatures with wings have the freedom and irresponsibility of the air. Human beings, equipped with hands, must use them to scrape holes in the earth. In putting down roots, we decide where we want to be buried. When Malouf published *Fly Away Peter* in 1982, he was one of the commuting birds he described: he lived in Tuscany, 'returning to Australia'— as the book's biographical note put it—'for a few months each year'. He has since shed his wings, sold his Tuscan property, and lives in Sydney all year round. Poets may envy skylarks and nightingales, but a novelist, who needs to understand life on the ground, should probably not be a frequent flyer.

The trenches in *Fly Away Peter* are described as a 'world upside down': the true Antipodes, but located—as a neat revenge—in the north. At Ypres, as at Gallipoli, the Australian recruits were reduced to troglodytes, subterranean gnomes.

Even in peacetime, England sentenced young Aussie travellers to the same fate by stowing them in cellars. In Henry Handel Richardson's novel, Richard Mahony moves from London to Leicester because his mother-in-law's house is 'not cursed with a basement'. But his surgery is still a couple of steps below street level, and a poky parlour—nicknamed the 'Black Hole'—offers an unappetising view of 'a walled-in yard no bigger than a roofless prison cell'. It's as if a folk memory of the trenches persists in the Australian mind. Shortly before her death in 1983, the novelist Christina Stead described her physiological distaste for London. It is 'built on mud', she said; she preferred cities with 'a rocky basis', like Sydney or New York. Murray Bail, living in central London during the early 1970s, found himself sinking into this quagmire of clay. In his notebook he glumly described his demotion: 'Langham Street. Two rooms, basement. Looking up I can see the ankles of English people pass.' Certainly no-one in Australia has such a downtrodden viewpoint. But that, after all, is what it means to be Antipodean: the feet opposed to you are thrust into your face.

Given this resentment, travel becomes the prosecution of our quarrel with the rest of the world. My fellow runaway Kate Jennings, who now lives in New York, remarks that the Australian abroad combines egomania with low self-esteem. The same mixture, she notes, is often found in drunkards. I think that's too harsh. I'd say that the Australian abroad is guarded, chippy, determined not to surrender too easily. Visiting Athens,

Tales of Two Hemispheres

the poet RF Brissenden climbs the Acropolis, then decides that it's a less sacred mound than Uluru. The blood-coloured monolith in the desert is our true church, and its gods, he believes, are preferable to the squabbling philanderers of Olympus. Kate Jennings in an autobiographical story describes a bus trip from London to Greece, at the end of which she glances at Olympus and mocks Zeus with his uncontrollable prick. All the same, she approves of Athens: 'The pavements are made of marble but everything smells of shit'. It is a uniquely Australian reason for valuing the ancient world. In our salubrious post-war suburbs, fresh linen circulated on rotary clothes lines and knights on white chargers purified your washing. I was never allowed to leave the house without a clean, ironed handkerchief in my pocket. By contrast, the encrusted grime of Europe reeked of romance; history for us meant soiling, stains, stench. Only an Australian could have reacted as Barry Humphries did when he first approached Venice. He ignored the shimmering visual mirage, and instead inhaled the odour of the stagnant canals. Civilisation could be defined as a place where it's not safe to drink the water.

Australians abroad are pilgrims intent on losing their faith not confirming it. They delight in disproving Europe's sense of priority. Jill Ker Conway, the historian who began life on a sheep station in rural New South Wales, was unimpressed by the breath-taking view from Montserrat, in the mountains above Barcelona: she preferred the 'mystical sense of oneness with nature' she enjoyed in the back country at home. When Americans tell the story of hemispherical collision, the emissary from the New World—typically called Newman, like the hero of Henry James's novel *The American*—is liable to be captivated and destroyed by wily Europeans. We are less naive, and less resigned to defeat. Some young Australians visiting Europe in a story by David Malouf are irritated by the wide-eyed wonderment of an American companion, who is 'foolishly impressed by everything foreign and picturesque'. Carrying grudges in their backpacks, the Australians are unlikely to be seduced by an old world they have not forgiven for abusing their ancestors.

In England during the 1970s, Murray Bail jotted down reports on this contest of wills with a culture that expected him to be overwhelmed and intimidated. A sign on a house near Berkeley Square boasts that it was built in 1759. Bail transcribes the plaque in his notebook, then snarls 'So what?' Quite right too: why should antiquity expect automatic veneration? In his novel *Homesickness*, about a group of Australians on a trip around the world, Bail derides London's complacent assumption that it is the centre of the world. His characters stay in a hotel annexed to the British Museum, so they're absorbed into its hoard of pillaged imperial trophies. Their postal address is WC2, and Bail insists on believing that the initials refer not to West Central but to water closet. The planners of the penal colony treated Australia as a conveniently distant cloaca; Bail in retaliation mistakes London for a toilet. Despite the allocation of postal zones, the city's centre is deserted when the offices close: England not Australia is the country with a dead heart. He also notices that the façade of Buckingham Palace is sooty, in need of a good scrubbing.

No opportunity for self-assertion is passed up. In his published notebook, *Longhand*, Bail takes offence at a tourist guide who asks his assembled herd 'Do you all speak English?' A sarcastic voice replies 'Can you manage Australian?' On another occasion, Bail goes on an excursion to Oxford. He stomps through the colleges, talking too loudly and blowing his nose unnecessarily—anything to make the hushed cloisters crassly echo. It's his way of defying the sclerosis of tradition. I doubt that Jill Ker Conway has ever blown her nose in public, but in 1958 she used it to sniff with when she first saw the English countryside. Even the supposedly desolate waste of Salisbury Plain seemed pocket-sized, trivial; the Australian landscape had formed the ground of her consciousness, and she could not accustom herself to a world without its spareness, vacancy and clarity. In a poem by Les Murray about a trip to Wales, this confrontation goes beyond the exchange of barbed put-downs. The opening of Murray's 'Vindaloo in Merthyr Tydfil' might have been written by one of Malouf's migrant birds: flying north, the poet imagines himself 'ascending the left cheek of Earth'—a lovely image that sees the planet as a rotund, well-fed face, and somehow makes the globe seem friendly. But on arrival, Murray feels obliged to hoist the flag. At an Indian restaurant, 'vain of my nation', he orders the hottest curry on the menu. The waiter tries to warn him against the vindaloo. Too proud to back down, Murray spoons the sulphurous goo into himself, sweats, gasps, croaks, and then, covered with spots, passes out beneath the upside-down Celtic stars. Still, he succeeds in cleaning his plate, and thus salvages Australia's honour (which really oughtn't to depend on his consumption of curry). The poem is wonderfully funny in its sketch of our toey aggressiveness when we find ourselves overseas and out of our trees. Like those deluded diggers in 1914, we spoil for a fight—and even a food fight will do.

Europeans, before they all recently began to fantasise about moving to Australia, used to enjoy ridiculing its paltry history. But we have learned not to allow them the last laugh. A story by Frank Moorhouse mentions a conference of Michelin Guide editors in Geneva. The assembled experts decide for the umpteenth time that Australia doesn't deserve its own guide book, since it lacks Benedictine abbeys and Gothic cathedrals. Why haven't the Aboriginal people bestirred themselves to build any picturesque ruins during their fifty thousand years of residence? Our museums are also poor, they complain, in 'blood-stained uniforms of archdukes'. This reference to the archduke's assassination at Sarajevo, which touched off World War I, revives our immemorial grudge against Europe, and suggests that history is something we are lucky to lack.

In the film version of the Barry McKenzie comic strip, written by Barry Humphries and Bruce Beresford in 1972, newspaper headlines offer intermittent updates on a leprosy epidemic that is supposedly ravaging England. It's the ideal disease with which to afflict a mouldering country. The guileless McKenzie is of course immune, as he blunders through a palsied Old World. Whenever a stately leper sneers about the bumptious colonies, Bazza unlocks his jutting jaw and mobilises his mouth in self-defence. A chinless wimp insults him at a dance organised by some oxymoronic Young Conservatives. 'May all your chooks turn to emus and kick your dunny down,' says our hero. 'Go dip your eye in hot cocky cack.' His hosts are dumbstruck when their language is used against them with such slangy glee.

The refined aesthete Barry Humphries has acclimatised himself to English society, but the monsters he gestates rampage on his behalf and terrorise the toffs. In 2002 Dame Edna popped up at a public concert held in the Buckingham Palace gardens to mark the Queen's golden jubilee. Moonee Ponds housewives know more than monarchs about the care of nature strips, so the self-appointed Dame reduced the actual Queen to an inept, awkward guest in her own backyard by warning that the hordes of picnickers would leave her lawns in a shocking state. (To think that the British tabloids frothed so indignantly when Paul Keating—in a much milder act of lése-majesté—merely laid his commoner's hand on the Queen's back to propel her through a crowd in Canberra!) That evening at the palace, Humphries multiplied himself to stage a two-pronged assault on the citadel of propriety and its unamused tenant. While Dame Edna dispensed green-fingered wisdom around the back, the cameras switched to the front of the building to report on a breach of security: Sir Les Patterson raged at the locked gates, slobbering and burping as he demanded admittance to the party. Early in the 1960s, Barry Humphries lost his footing on a Cornish cliff, tumbled backwards, and had to be hauled up from a precarious ledge above the sea. He had, as he put it, fallen off England—though really the aim of his satire is to push England itself over the edge.

The British Empire once rallied its loyal minions for use as cannon fodder; now the conscripts break ranks and form a fifth column to sabotage their smug hosts. Hence the satyr play staged at the Palace by Edna and Les, or—not far off—the brothel opened in Chelsea by the androgynous Eadith in Patrick White's *The Twyborn Affair*. She attends to the kinky sexual requirements of courtiers and Cabinet ministers, and thus (in White's phrase) services 'a society determined on its own downfall'. In post-colonial times, there can be no prouder work. White felt himself to be 'temperamentally a cosmopolitan Londoner', and pretended that residence in Australia was a punitive exile. But his cantankerous choice of allegiance didn't prevent him from relishing England's degeneration during the strike-ridden 1970s. As garbage stank in the streets and power stations shut, he rejoiced: the sleazier London became, he said, the more at home he felt.

The same war of self-vindication has been prosecuted across the Atlantic by Robert Hughes. He remembers the beached impatience of young Australians in the 1950s, pacing to and fro during their long wait for reports from the hemisphere where modernism was happening. He and his cronies scanned the horizon for copies of the magazine *ARTnews*, which drifted across the ocean by sea mail, bringing fuzzy small-scale reproductions of paintings by the New York Abstract Expressionists. Writers shared this sense of relegation to Bullamakanka. As a character in a Frank Moorhouse story puts it, Meanjin is an 'Aboriginal word meaning "rejected from *The New Yorker*"'. After two decades in New York as art critic of *Time*, Hughes toppled the conceited city in a poem called *The SoHoiad*—a pastiche on *The Dunciad*, in which Alexander Pope assaulted the illiterate litterateurs of eighteenth-century London. Paraphrasing the end of Pope's mock-epic, Hughes wishes destruction on hype-inflated Manhattan and its loud-mouthed poseurs. Pope prescribed the onset of apocalyptic darkness, an uncreating night. Hughes, more ribald, unleashes a volcanically eruptive fart, then adds a coda of personal triumph:

> The Antipodean Shepherd drops his gaze,
> Brings to an end his Apopemptick Lays,
> Resigns his Doric flute, and hopes for better days.

By blowing their noses or by breaking wind, Australians can shake the foundations of those fabled northern cities. But what happens when the campaign of subversion is over, and the time comes to return south? In Patrick White's *A Fringe of Leaves*, the ship bringing Mrs Roxburgh back from England to Van Diemen's Land is wrecked off Queensland; living with the Aborigines, she unlearns the civilised habits of the northern hemisphere and patiently awaits the time when her skeleton, 'blessed with its final inarticulate white', will sift into the stone and dust of 'this country to which it can at last belong'. She imagines her bleached remains fertilising the land. That acceptance was easier for her than for White. The skeleton, he says, is 'inarticulate': homecoming requires you to die, and of course to stop writing.

Some of us came to think of re-entry as a kind of death, an enforced transportation to a home we expected never to see again. In 1899 Henry Lawson urged young Australian writers to stow away or swim to Blighty or Yankeeland, since the only alternative to expatriation was suicide. In 1921, after a spell in London, the literary critic Vance Palmer made the retrograde decision to go back to Australia. His friend Louis Esson congratulated him on his courage, treating repatriation as a noble martyrdom: 'You did the heroic thing in returning'. Esson also urged Palmer to escape to London again as soon he could. When Melba retired to Melbourne, she dolefully exchanged the 'big world'—with its pelted bouquets, titled lovers and private railway carriages—for a world that was smaller, more innocuously domestic. But she hinted that she wouldn't refuse if her itsy-bitsy native land sent her back on the road as a roving diplomat.

Surely the rite of passage between hemispheres is not as traumatic as the trip through the birth canal, or the journey from this world to the next? In 1999 Murray Bail, characteristically contrary, demystified the life-changing voyage north that we all used to take. He did so by the simple tactic of reversing it, travelling back to Australia from England on a container ship. He probably chose the vessel because its name was *Romance*. There was nothing romantic about it, but that, for Bail, was the point: the journey was an exercise in boredom, an apprenticeship to inertia. Geography today is virtual, and space is no longer graded and segregated. We can stop thinking of ourselves as provincials, and don't need to plan pilgrimages to the omphalos; we must also do without the intense, emotionally churning ceremonies of departure and arrival that used to mark the stages of our personal evolution.

As the only passenger on the *Romance*, Bail spends an immured month traipsing round in circles on the deck. Occasionally, remembering that he's a writer, he describes a sunrise or a rainbow in his diary. His Australian landfall elicits no rhetorical fanfares. Germaine Greer apparently expects to be smoked when she descends from the sky, and cools her heels at the airport until an indigenous matriarch officially welcomes her. Bail, however, rolls out no red carpet for himself. In Fremantle, wharfies shout across the water as they grapple with the ropes that will yoke his ship to the continent. Bail concludes his diary by recording their raillery, worth salvaging because these are the 'first words from Australia'. The words turn out to be 'Fuckun idiots!' When Bail hears that, he knows he is home. I hope he allowed himself to smile as he descended the gangplank.

five
Austerica

I begin with another shamefaced admission: it was in America that I first realised how much I missed Australia. The recognition was accidental, even reluctant, and like many of our most convulsive emotions it entered my head through my nose. I was on the cliffs above the ocean outside San Francisco, where the western world, having piled up a last crest of skyscrapers on hills made wobbly by a seismic fault, suddenly comes to an end. Fog choked the Golden Gate, and a squall passed over. To escape a drenching, I sheltered in a clump of trees. When the rain stopped, I wondered why I didn't resume my walk. Something detained me, tugged me into my past. I looked up and saw that the trees I was standing under were eucalypts, which had released their oily, pungent aroma into the wet air. Like a dog, I was smelling my way home.

Of course it was a deceptive epiphany. For as long as the sensation lasted, I was in the imaginary land of Austerica, which is an ugly word for a muddled idea: a conflation of Australia and America. I knew my way around this synthetic place, because—

like everyone else in my generation—I had already spent a fair proportion of my mental life there. My first passport defined me as an Australian citizen and a British subject. It didn't mention my subjection to a mythical, imperious America.

As a boy, I signed up for the contagious American fantasy by playing games of cowboys and Indians in a suburban Hobart street. We used imaginary weapons, but quarrelled furiously over exactly when the non-existent bullets and arrows (always accompanied with stereophonic sound effects) were fatal. I never minded being killed, because it presented the opportunity for spectacular falls and gurgling last gasps. Toolsheds were redefined as besieged garrisons in the desert, and a pile of cardboard boxes could be a circle of wagons under assault. For scenery, a back fence sufficed, so long as gunfire could be exchanged over it. A dusty street would have been ideal, but bitumen was acceptable. We were under strict instructions not to die on our parents' lawns or to trample their flower beds. I envied the would-be Indians next door when they appeared with home-made head-dresses of chicken feathers: eagles, turkeys and even owls, whose feathers the American natives preferred, were unavailable. In those days the local homage to the Davey Crockett hat—using rabbit fur, since we also lacked racoons and beavers—was the most prized of Christmas presents.

The first American friend I ever had, during my time as a student at Oxford, said to me with something like pity, 'You know, it must be really weird to grow up outside the States'. The remark now seems to me quite sinister, since his assumption was that childhood depended on access to American television and American TV snacks. The sad thing is that I knew exactly what he meant, and could confirm the truth of it.

Throughout Australia's history, it has been periodically exhorted to Americanise itself. Developers early in the twentieth century recommended the American example: fill up the continent with those poor, huddled masses who were welcomed to New York by the Statue of Liberty, and send them off to tear wealth from the land. Unfortunately our arid, eroded terrain resisted exploitation. Having failed to equal the United States, we begged to be allowed to join it. After the British deserted Singapore, the Curtin government looked to Roosevelt and General MacArthur for protection. The hurried change of allegiance left us feeling abject. Mary Kent Hughes of the RA Medical Corps remembered a conversation in 1942 with an AIF officer stationed in Darwin. 'What a pity that they [the Americans] had to be landed in this hole!' he said. 'They will get the impression that Australia is not worth fighting for!' All we could offer in return was our obsequious reliability as client state, which is why we so promptly signed up for America's military adventures in Vietnam and Iraq.

We may share a community of interest, but we have little else in common with America. Historical experience, political doctrine and national character divide us. The Americans mechanically abridged their slice of the continent. An iron horse puffed from east to west; a golden spike was driven into the married rails. Our self-mocking domestic equivalent to America's invincible locomotive is the platoon of lawnmowers that shaved the Astroturf in the stadium during the opening ceremony of the Sydney Olympics. Though Americans believed they were living in God's own country, they soon rearranged its nature, lavishing water stolen from the Colorado River on the pampered gardens of Los Angeles. The Australian interior proved more intractable, and killed off most of those who set out to explore it. Economic success accounts for the triumphalism of the American character, with its chatter about goals, dreams, and being the best you can be. Baffled or humbled by the land, we are disinclined to be boastful. A little verse in a book called *Stand Easy*, handed out to demobbed soldiers like my father in 1946, sums up our more phlegmatic temperament. In what it calls an 'Australian Charter', it advises against boasting about victory or deprecating 'the ways that are not ours'. We should not 'strive for fame', but rather humbly 'let other men assess what we have done'. The flaunting poppy is warned to lower its head, for fear of decapitation:

> … should we reap, in time, some measure of applause,
> Or reach the path that leads towards the crest of fame,
> Beware! Lest paltry pomp divert us from our course
> And send us toppling back from whence we came.

It's hard to imagine an American Johnny marching home again to such a muffled tune.

Austerica

In many ways we remain closer psychologically to our European origins—half Irish, half Mediterranean—than we are to the race of new, brash beings propagated by nascent America. The convicts are our founding fathers, so we think of ourselves as disruptive rascals, honorary felons; in the long run, it's probably better to descend from petty criminals and scalliwags than from messianic puritans. David Malouf sensed an affinity with the sharp-minded, witty Tuscan villagers who used to be his neighbours. 'A vigorous scepticism rather than passion,' as he said, '[is] the leading characteristic of most Mediterranean minds.' The same is true of Australian minds. We're content to leave passion—at least of the ideological kind—to Americans. Other aspects of Mediterranean consciousness have made the journey south. As Norman Lindsay pointed out, Pan the lewd satyr emigrated from Greece or Italy to Australia, where hedonism has become a religion—except that, wiser than the Americans, we know that happiness is not something you should exhaustingly pursue. John Updike defines America as 'a vast conspiracy to make you happy' (or at least, as the mourners dolefully repeated during Ronald Reagan's funeral, to make you feel good about yourself). It's a conspiracy because the happiness America dispenses must be purchased. So long as you have money, you can get fast food, carbonated drinks, Prozac, cocaine, Viagra, innumerable channels of trash beamed into your brain from a satellite, and a pin embossed with the stars and stripes to wear above your heart. Happiness in

Tales of Two Hemispheres

Australia is a simpler matter, the by-product of the climate, our benign coasts, and a mentality that might be called happy-go-lucky. We know we're privileged, but we don't confuse our good fortune with merit. Nor, I hope, do we equate enjoyment with conspicuous consumption. And we ration the quantity of bliss we allow ourselves. 'Well, I'm happy enough here' was my father's mantra: he could never understand why I needed to leave home in order to be happier.

America is fuelled by a faith that toxically mixes puritanism and capitalism, 'personal growth' (as the self-help manuals call it) and financial gain. With our different notion of the good life, it's hard for us not to mistrust that blend of righteous zeal and propulsive energy. Richard Flanagan in his novel *Gould's Book of Fish* refers to Americans as 'endearing question marks of human beings'. They resemble the punctuation mark both spiritually and physically: they're always bending down from their great height to ask us whether we love them. Of course, like the scurrilous underdogs we are, we give them the answer they want to hear. Flanagan is thinking of the credulous Americans who disembark from cruise ships in Hobart to inspect the craft shops on Salamanca Place, where—he jokes—they buy Shaker furniture that has actually been made by Vietnamese boat people.

Joan Colebrook, who grew up outside Cairns in the 1930s, initially looked askance at an American Foreign Service official she met in Brisbane. In his striped seersucker suit, he had—as she says in her memoir, *House of Trees*—'that eager, slightly naive look which I had always associated with facsimiles of such young men in the advertisements in American magazines.' When he proposed to her, she realised that she could never share his flighty notion of 'life as an open highway on which we could both proceed together without any possible hindrance'—an existential Route 66. She married him all the same, although the match sounds less like a meeting of minds than a coalition of the vaguely willing. She found the relationship convenient and undemanding, because 'he came from a less critical culture—a culture that was more pliable and easygoing than ours'. Pliable and easygoing or perhaps, on the contrary, rampantly self-willed, unwilling to concede that others think differently? You can quibble about Colebrook's diplomatic choice of adjectives, but she's astute in noting the strains in any Austerican alliance. Self-celebration is not our mode. Her own doubts, as Colebrook says in describing her childhood in the rainforest, were bred by loneliness. The scorching, metallic sky was a reminder of her insignificance and the irrelevance of the society to which she belonged, uncomfortably unpacked in a jungle.

On their open highway, Americans don't bother looking in the rear-view mirror. This too marks one of the defining differences between us. Judith Wright recalls meeting an American who told her that he was shocked by Australia's preoccupation with its injurious past: the brutality of the penal colony, the extermination of the Aboriginal people. In America, the casualties of progress are quickly forgotten. Why brood over your beginnings, when the constitution guarantees you the right to reinvent yourself? Plastic surgery is available for the soul; there is room enough for you to move on and start all over again. Australians lack this convenient amnesia. We remain preoccupied by the primal scenes of settlement here, anxious to understand what happened and perhaps to make amends. In their Boyer lectures, Inga Clendinnen and David Malouf both began from Australia's fraught origins: a violent encounter between a French naturalist and an Aboriginal woman on a beach in western Australia in 1801, or—less threateningly—a performance of Shakespeare's *Henry IV* given by convicts in Sydney the year before. The incident on the beach dramatised by Clendinnen sets the agenda for our subsequent history of racial conflict; the entertainment described by Malouf alleviates conflict by transforming it into play. Memory, in both cases, is the medium of conscience. Our retrospectiveness may impede our go-getting, but that's to our moral credit.

America's manifest destiny has always been to universalise itself. After the railway linked the east and west coasts, Walt Whitman extended the victorious trajectory across the Pacific by fantasising about a passage to India—or perhaps, veering south, to Australia. Then and now, the purpose was conversion and co-optation, to turn other countries into mimicries of America and markets for its wares. Clinging to the shores of our overgrown island, we have always sought a connection to the rest of the world, perhaps because we were told that we'd been expelled from it. America is less curious, and copes with what's left of the globe by buying it up: London Bridge spans a lake in the Arizona desert, the Houses of Parliament at Westminster are rebuilt in black glass in Pittsburgh, Venice and Paris are resurrected inside Las Vegas casinos. In 1966 in Saigon, John Pilger checked out a GI bar called Dreamland, lit by purple neon with a thudding jukebox and an air conditioner set to a polar temperature. Its smashed customers had no idea where in the world they were; they dealt with disorientation by making believe they were at a truck stop beside a highway in the American Midwest. To conquer the world, you don't need to know anything about it. Ignorance may even be an advantage, since it smooths away complexities.

There's an anecdotal warning of the danger to us in Robert Altman's film *Buffalo Bill and the Indians*. Paul Newman plays Buffalo Bill, an old fraud whose shabby mystique is bolstered by an itinerant circus troupe of impostors. Two Australians turn up and ask for a job in Bill's Wild West show. When he casts them as Mexicans, they protest. Pointing out that they have blue eyes, they plead to be allowed to play Tasmanians: isn't that exotic enough? But they're summarily renamed Manuel and Muñoz, whether they like it or not. Americans have always had designs on our outback, which they envisage as a sort of Texas stocked with kangaroos instead of coyotes. Hence the mongrelised Westerns made here by actors who couldn't get better jobs in California: Kirk Douglas in *The Man from Snowy River*, Tom Selleck culling dingos in *Quigley Down Under*. We should all be grateful to RM Williams, the manufacturer of elastic-sided boots, for establishing the integrity of our unAmerican frontier. In his plans for the Australian Stockman's Hall of Fame in Longreach, Queensland, Williams prohibited any reference to cowboys. 'That's American,' he decreed. 'It means boys who milk the cow. Call 'em stockmen.' The Marlboro Man, for all his posturing, is merely a jumped-up milkmaid, and Australians have a prior claim to virility. National identity and self-determination depend on such quibbles.

In the summer of 1958 Sidney Nolan, visiting the United States on a Harkness Fellowship, drove around the country. His expedition was less a holiday than an exercise in comparative anthropology, since he wanted to examine the differences between American and Australian myths. In Lincoln County, New Mexico, he attended a rustic pageant commemorating Billy the Kid, because he was intrigued by the analogy with our martyred outlaw Ned Kelly. The two, he discovered, were unrelated. Billy the career killer was motivated by mental derangement and a craving for celebrity. The legend served as an excuse for a theatrical shoot-out in which Americans noisily exercised their right to bear arms. This display of lawlessness showed Nolan how different Ned Kelly was—game but reluctant to shed blood, a good loser who has endeared himself to Australians because of his grimly nonchalant fatalism. On the road, Nolan came to understand the rage that drove America's idealism. Even the jazz trumpeters in New Orleans blew, he said, 'as if to bring down the walls of Jericho' or to impel 'a migration of angels. Pigmented ones'. Americans were motorised millenarians, pursuing happiness at sixty miles an hour without needing to shift gear, speeding towards that convulsive moment when the dreams of the righteous would come true and God would descend to fraternise with his chosen people. Australian space, however, does not open into a promised land; our deserts place a cautionary limit on aspiration.

During his trip Nolan made a detour to visit Patrick White, then grumpily resident among the orange groves in Florida. The purpose was to discuss his cover design for White's novel, *The Aunt's Story*, which ends with an aborted journey across America. On her way home from the disintegrating Europe of the 1930s, the mad aunt travels through the Midwest by train. She is irritated by a fellow passenger in a laundered shirt, who chews popcorn and regales her with statistics about the exponentiating populations of Chicago and Kansas City. The one-sided conversation reminds Theodora of 'the difference between doing and being'—which corresponds, perhaps, to that between industrious America and her own contemplative Australia. She too, like Voss, is an Australian explorer, though she does her travelling inside her head. She compliments her American hosts for making life 'positively pneumatic', but she cannot believe in their spiritual hydraulics or their mechanistic provision for a 'reasonable life'. She therefore steps off the train in New Mexico, leaving it to steam on 'with all its magnificence of purpose, to California'.

The opposition White finds between the hemispheres is a cosmic clash of light and dark. Theo grows up a property called

Meroë, named after a classical prototype. When she notices that they have only a creek not the Nile, her father tells her that 'There is another Meroë, a dead place, in the black country of Ethiopia.' Rejecting brightness, she travels in quest of the dark on the globe's other side. Hence her distaste for utilitarian America, which she envisages as 'a small, white, placid heap', a lump of numbers. But her addled brain muddles the hemispheres, so in announcing that she is on her way home she tells her relatives that she is coming back to Abyssinia, not Australia. It's a revealing error: she may be referring to Samuel Johnson's *Rasselas*, a fable about an Abyssinian prince who lives in a happy valley, leaves it in search of a better life, then slopes home, depressed and disappointed. Or does she mean that Australia is an abyss, by contrast with the superficiality of America? Either way, she never gets there. At the beginning of the novel, she is astonished by the way cuts heal on the bare knees of two boys. Their bodies, she sees, 'denied the myth of putrefaction'. Theo herself chooses decay, preferring the boneyard to the clinic. A kindly doctor takes her to a white room, but she is beyond the help of American medicine, which assumes that all unhappiness can be cured by a pill or a therapist.

When Australia invented its own variant of the American epic in George Miller's *Mad Max*, a combination of Western and road movie, the film was required to lie about its source. Before it could be distributed in the United States, it had to sacrifice its Australian accent and its salty slang: Mel Gibson and the others

Austerica

were dubbed by Americans. The imposture couldn't conceal the film's oddity, or the jaunty despair that made it so Australian. *Mad Max* is set in the future, after a nuclear war has left civil society and its protocols in disarray. But actually it reverts to the past and re-imagines the scenery of Australia's earliest years: a moral waste, populated by hoons in souped-up jalopies with leather-clad enforcers giving chase. No American frontier shines in the distance, as alluring as gold. Instead there is only a strip of tarmac painted with the skull and crossbones. The first chase is along Anarchie Road, past a sign announcing the presence of the Main Force Patrol: an anonymous Australian wit has changed Force to Farce, which sums up the savage hilarity of our world-view. For Joan Colebrook's American husband in *House of Trees*, the highway conducts you directly towards gratification. Australians see the thoroughfare differently: in *Mad Max* it is littered with road kill, and after an accident in which a cop is slashed in the throat and loses his voice box, the terse message to the emergency services is, 'Better send the meat truck'. Life is a mincer, and we're all just waiting to be ground into kangaroo patties. But the citizens of this terminal world are buoyantly good-humoured. A young couple speed away from the brutalised town of Wee Jerusalem where the thugs are staging drag races. 'No worries,' says the young man, with a brave grin; at that instant, a feral marauder carves open the roof of their car with a hatchet. The Antipodean vision persists, depriving victims of their dignity. Max's mate Goose flails helplessly, strapped into his inverted car as petrol leaks from the engine. 'Look at him,' sniggers the villainous Toecutter's catamite, 'he looks silly upside down!'

Apart from occasional glimpses of the West Gate Bridge in Melbourne and the city's drab brick-veneer suburbs, the terrain in the film is parched and discoloured, abstractly featureless, as if ironed level. The aesthetics of flatness are inimitably Australian: the drawling, even-toned eloquence of local speech, trickling out through half-open mouths, or (as Peter Sculthorpe points out) the slow rate of harmonic change and elongated pedal notes in our music, exemplified by the didgeridoo. This horizontality has always puzzled and offended Americans. Herbert Hoover, later a disastrous American President during the Depression, came to Coolgardie and Kalgoorlie as a mining engineer in the 1890s. He described the country as 'unbelievably flat and uninteresting. There is not a fish in stretches of a thousand miles.' With no Rocky Mountains to cross, or wildlife to be shot or reeled in, where was the sense of achievement? Hoover demoted the roads to mere 'tracks', which 'added to the monotony of life'. They hardly resembled American highways, speeding into the lucrative future. His bafflement is a reminder that Americans saw their wilderness as something to be assaulted, subjugated. The epigraph to Cecil B de Mille's *Union Pacific* calls the West 'America's empire', and celebrates the railway for opening a trade-route. The film *How the West Was Won* concludes by admitting that the frontier has been closed, but vaults prophetically ahead in an aerial survey of the Boulder Dam, agribusiness around Salinas, and the Los Angeles freeways; the camera finally swoops through the Golden Gate, embarking on the mercantile passage to India. The society of *Mad Max* offers no prospect of expansion and enrichment. Australians are squeezed between two inhospitable infinities, one dry, the other wet. Max does battle on the edge of the desert, then retires to meditate revenge on the beach, moodily staring at a cold wintry ocean on the Mornington Peninsula.

Travel is a paradoxical business—supposedly outgoing, in fact self-obsessed. We travel to see people who are different from us, which means that our real aim must be to discover our own singularity. Sometimes, unexpectedly, there is no difference. On a visit to Benares, Murray Bail observed that India is 'where you are reminded that you are naturally the same as everyone else'. The experience of Asia is immersive; it obliterates the personal solitude we are taught to treasure and to defend. America does the opposite. Individualism is the country's creed, but exposure to all those clamorous, world-beating egos startles you into the realisation that the self, for Australians, is not necessarily a guided missile.

In *Homesickness*, Murray Bail doubles the available hemispheres as his band of intrepid Australians travels round the world. He begins with northern and southern hemispheres, renamed Greater and Lesser. The upper hemisphere monopolises 'tall rectangles' and has the lion's share of the landmass; the hemisphere below consists merely of water, heat and raw materials, and its inhabitants spend their time, staring enviously upwards, as you do at New York skyscrapers. But a vertical division can also be made, which leaves you with two other hemispheres, left and right. These are the complementary halves of the brain, and they correspond—on Bail's whimsical map—to the matching, competing continents of America and Europe. Affections and manias, images and words have their home on the right, that is in Europe. Across the Atlantic is the left hemisphere, devoted to engines and equations, angular and logically organised. New York in Bail's novel is a barrage of machinery. Even the clouds glimpsed in crevices between buildings above Wall Street are sliced into exiguous triangles.

As jackhammers rattle the ground and 747s screech overhead, one of the travellers in *Homesickness* suddenly recognises that Australians are quiet and self-contained people, averse to making a noise in the world. Americans have a verbal confidence that they perhaps inherited from the sermonising fanatics who founded their country. 'Our sentences are shorter,' says Violet. 'Our thoughts break off.' Borelli agrees: 'We speak in jerks.' Does the empty land push its way into our sentences, inserting pauses and dead ends, allowing trails to run dry? Unlike the Americans, we are also given to fatuous, matey banter, and this too might be a psychological quirk, another reflex of our territorial fate. 'Quips keep us going,' suggests Borelli. 'Being so far removed and relatively alone, we seem to need encouragement. Quips help us along; things aren't all that bad. It's as if, in Australia, we're all in hospital. There's a lot of quipping in hospital.' Indignantly patriotic, Mrs Cathcart reminds him that 'Sir Robert Menzies was a fine speaker'. Since the oratory of Menzies was mostly wind, this bluster may prove Borelli's point.

Patrick White in *The Cockatoos* tartly comments on that tone of 'contralto seriousness in which American women specialise'. Sooner our halting, dubious language than the glib rhetoric and megaphonic hectoring that comes so naturally to Americans; irony is preferable to zeal. Bail's characters agree that Americans are the master race, but only because they control the means of communication. 'They've had television for a long time,' someone says. It might be added that Americans now all behave as if they were on television, auditioning for guest appearances on some wisecracking sitcom or for confessional interviews on a therapeutic talk show. Rupert Murdoch is our gift to this new world: an Australian who acquired American nationality so he'd be eligible to own a television network.

Edward Heath, the Tory leader deposed by Margaret Thatcher, once told me about a flying visit he made to Melbourne in 1967 to attend the memorial service for Harold Holt. President Johnson also turned up, posthumously rewarding Holt for his compliance over Vietnam. LBJ lumbered out of his bulletproof limo and swaggered into the cathedral, surrounded by a phalanx of security guards. One muscle-bound minder carried the box of nuclear codes, just in case Johnson needed to blow the world up during the service. When Prince Charles arrived, Johnson rose from his pew and fulsomely welcomed him to Australia. Charles—still a teenager but clearly itching for his inheritance—said, 'Thank you Mr President, but since this is my country, let me welcome you'. I wish someone had got up and contradicted both of them by pointing out that the country belonged to itself, not to the rival potentates who had dropped in for the day.

In 1940 the expatriate novelist Martin Boyd urged Australia to seek military aid from the United States, and prophesied that its future lay with 'the new countries'. Boyd belonged to a Melbourne clan that considered itself to be Anglo-Australian, and had spent his childhood planning his escape to England; his own choice was irreversible, but now, as the war compelled nations to redefine their self-interest, he saw his mistake. 'A mother fixation', he admitted, was no more 'admirable nationally than individually.' It was a shrewd diagnosis of the Oedipus complex from which he and Australia both then suffered. We all have to be weaned, and must slice through the cord that attaches us to Mummy and her soothing traditional pieties. But it's not much healthier to be fixated on our belligerent big brother.

six
Oz

Landlocked in Tasmania, I remember groaning at the thought of all the water dumped around us. Bass Strait, I calculated, would be difficult enough to get across; after that, I'd still have to ford the Indian or Pacific Oceans before I could get anywhere. Today oceans have contracted to puddles, and the continents overlap in an electronic continuum. Gravity also used to feel oppressive, lowering us in the world's esteem. During my lifetime, Australia has cast off this impediment and floated northwards.

Nowadays it turns up everywhere. In Paris on the Left Bank of the Seine, opposite Notre Dame, there's a shop selling didgeridoos, Akubra hats and Drizabone coats, along with compact discs of soporific New Age noises from the rainforest. I assume that, deep in the Latin Quarter, a tribe of bushwhackers is smoking Gauloises and quarrelling about philosophy with gestures of unAustralian animation. In Antwerp, outside the cathedral, there's a hole in the wall with a sign advertising Australian ice-cream. I noticed this on a soaking day in December; the shop had no customers, and I don't remember whether there was anyone behind the counter, scoop at the ready. Maybe I dreamed it, or perhaps the dream was what the shop sold, a fantasy of southern warmth conjured up like a charm in the chilly north. In Lisbon, beside the Tagus, there's a concrete box with horns bristling around its roof and a yellow road sign in the window mendaciously announcing WOMBATS NEXT 10 MILES: the Outback Steakhouse. In a country where the staple dish is cod, what could be more exotic than charred beef?

Last year, among the blueberry muffins at Starbuck's in San Francisco, I was startled to see something labelled an 'Aussie cookie': imagine an Anzac biscuit fed on steroids and given chocolate chip implants. This was on Geary Street, across from a theatre where every afternoon a consignment of gladdies arrived at the stage door in a florist's van. Yes, Dame Edna happened to be in town. Yet only forty years before, up on Nob Hill, a few steep blocks away, Christopher Koch rented an apartment from a landlord who had to consult a wall map to ascertain Australia's whereabouts. He then complimented his new tenant on speaking the American language without all that much of a brogue.

The first thing I saw in Las Vegas, after getting off a plane earlier this year, was an assortment of my muscled compatriots preening in Y-fronts: a poster for Thunder From Down Under, a troupe of male strippers resident at one of the casinos. Every night they titillate gaggles of bachelorettes by shedding their spandex tights, which are ecumenically decorated with both Old Glory and the Southern Cross. Did Chesty Bond, who used to preen in an athletic vest during my boyhood, ever imagine that he might enjoy an international career as a dancing fetish? Meanwhile in England, the British with their callipygian tastes dote on Kylie Minogue's bottom—and Kylie, keen to preserve her bodily capital, recently threatened to sue a tabloid which printed a puffy, sagging close-up of someone else's rear and passed it off as hers. Exoticism has always implied erotic licence. Young Aussie blondes of both sexes deposit business cards in London telephone boxes, which these days—since no-one would do anything so daggy as make a phone call in one of them—function as bulletin boards for nubile imported flesh.

Other consumer items crowd the shelves in the supermarkets in London. Coffee from the Atherton Tablelands sells at a premium, and Jacob's Creek wine—having shrewdly sponsored the last seasons of *Friends*—has become essential equipment for yuppies who want to appear witty, convivial and cosmopolitan. The commercials cleverly disarmed British resentment of the upsurgent colonies. 'Just what we need—more Australians!' sighed the commentary. Then some bottles of Merlot slid across the screen: our wine is welcome, even if we're not. Struggling home during a week of snow and sleet last January, I noticed another plaintive ad on the bus shelter around the corner from my house. The space had been rented by Foster's, which was encouraging local observance of Australia Day. 'Party Like It's Summer!' shrieked a slogan. On the poster, a line-up of shivering, sniffling Britons in woolly hats and overcoats gripped lager cans

Tales of Two Hemispheres

in frostbitten hands that should have held mugs of cocoa. The image was a heartless Antipodean revenge, a reminder that, in another hemisphere, everyone was at the beach. I suspect that the promotion failed: some ironies are too cruel, even for long-suffering Londoners.

The more personal the item being sold, the more insidious is its appeal. For a long while, I bought all my clothes at Country Road on West Broadway in New York. It hardly mattered that the people doing the selling were Americans, or that the garments had been sobered up to suit Manhattan tastes. A rust-red shirt looked to me as if it had been peeled off the epidermis of Australia; the word merino on a label was irresistible. The shampoo I use has a mob of kangaroos bounding around the top of the flask; it justifies the image by insisting that kangaroo-paw flower is blended with the sulfates and sodium chloride. Next to it in my shower, I have to tell you, is a bottle of tea-tree conditioner. Consumerism caters to emotional cravings as well as to humdrum physical needs, and these products are all elixirs. Even so, a fair amount of duplicity underlies such efforts to merchandise Australia. The small print on my shampoo gives contact addresses in Ireland and the Netherlands, where kangaroos are not native, and it adds a warning that 'Aussie is a trademark'. Has some offshore corporation copyrighted our country?

At least we finally have what the marketing experts call name recognition. The adjective, for good or ill, is as potent as the wet eucalypts I smelled in San Francisco. Years later, I still can't get over my delight at a line of dialogue in the English television series *Queer as Folk*, when spotty Vince from Manchester reflects on his good luck in having been picked up by Cameron, a wet dream from down under. Vince doubts that he'll qualify for a second date. 'I can't be the best shag he's ever had,' he sighs. 'I mean, he's Australian!' The exclamation is positively erectile. It's equally telling when the word is used as a term of abuse. In *Intolerable Cruelty*, written and directed by the Coen brothers, Geoffrey Rush returns to his Hollywood house in the middle of the day and surprises his wife in bed with the pool boy. She clobbers him with the statuette he has won for producing a soap opera and screams, 'You Australian piece of shit!' The adjective is placed with witty precision, to intensify the insult: it's not the shit that is Australian but the Australian who is shitty.

Our new desirability is both gratifying and alarming. The marketers know that we're persuaded to reach for our credit cards by a fantasy. Products are sold by touting a reverie about the place to which they're supposed to transport us. New Zealand has relaunched itself as Middle Earth, painting the national airline's 747s with crusading knights and stunted elves; tourists are offered a trip to the kind of place that Tolkien called a 'secondary world'—a feudal theme park where magicians fend off modernity with their runes. We can't afford to scoff. Australia long ago redefined itself by adopting the imaginary setting of a Hollywood film. Hugh Jackman, impersonating the spangled dervish Peter Allen, introduced himself to his Broadway audiences this year by

Tales of Two Hemispheres

telling them that he was born in Australia—'better known to you as Oz'. The show was *The Boy from Oz*, a title with more of a bankable lilt than *The Boy from Australia*, and it made Australia look like a lurid tropical resort over-run by disco dancers, easily accessible from Kansas if you hopped aboard a tornado.

Lacking our own myth of origins, we borrow one from L Frank Baum's stories about the emerald city. In some ways, it fits. The Land of Oz retains its wonders, Baum says, because it has been 'cut off from all the rest of the world', isolated by deserts not (like Australia) by oceans. The dusty, monochrome Kansas where Dorothy lives with Auntie Em in *The Wizard of Oz* could be the fly-blown outback. David Williamson's play *Emerald City* re-routes the yellow brick road, which now leads to the skyline of Sydney with all its lustrous, treacherous enchantments. In Williamson's version of the myth, Kansas is Melbourne, the home of high seriousness. But the analogy with Oz is not flattering to us. Baum apparently gave his imaginary realm its name after glancing at the drawer in his filing cabinet labelled O–Z. Wilde's snooty duchess in *Lady Windermere's Fan*, having looked up Australia on the map, remarks that it resembles a packing case. The bottom drawer of Baum's filing cabinet is also a roomy vacancy. Australia remains an obliging void, into which distant admirers can stuff their daydreams.

Our new popularity comes at a price. We should not expect to be understood or even to be truly valued; our customers only want to add another country or culture or cuisine to their shopping list, and can't spare the time for anything but a facile sampling. In *The Moor's Last Sigh*, Salman Rushdie breathily evokes three exotic places: 'Shanghai! Montevideo! Alice Springs!' He then proposes that such locations 'only yield up their secrets, their profound mysteries, to those who are just passing through'. Imagine his outrage if one of us said the same about Bombay! Rushdie kept Bruce Chatwin company in the Northern Territory while Chatwin was quizzing the locals about Aboriginal lore; perhaps that's why he decided that Australia and its mythological wisdom could be crammed into your head in a hurry. In 2004 Philip Glass composed an equally brisk global symphony entitled *Orion* for the Athens Olympics. Its succession of auditory stop-overs featured separate and then simultaneous performances by the Indian sitar, the Chinese pipa, the Gambian kora, the Gaelic fiddle and, of course, the didgeridoo. Each of those instruments is meant to speak in dialect, or perhaps in one of the secret Aboriginal languages that are known only to a closed community; it's dismaying to think of them merged in the kind of unidiomatic Esperanto used by airline employees. People used to say that music was international because it avoided language and enunciated pure emotion. Now music is global, and has a different responsibility: rather than superseding language, it must be fluent in all tongues at once.

At a concert in London in 1996, I realised how much can be lost in translation. The Brodsky Quartet, augmented by the Swedish mezzo-soprano Anne Sofie von Otter, was playing Peter Sculthorpe's *Island Dreaming*. The Brodskys—dumpy Mancunians, despite the Russian name they've adopted—did their best to make their stringed instruments sound ethnic. Von Otter, a patrician blonde with a voice of arctic whiteness, gamely sight-read a tribal incantation and a refrain about rowing out to the reef to fish, both written in some outlandish language. When I looked in the concert programme, I found that the words Sculthorpe set came from 'the Tallest Straight Islands north of Australia'. I couldn't imagine where these tall straight islands might be, or what they might look like. Perhaps they resembled von Otter, a six-footer with immaculate posture and spikily upright hair. Then I realised that Tallest Straight was a misprint for Torres Strait. Had someone telephoned Sculthorpe in Sydney and misunderstood his accent?

Despite the howler, it was good to hear a Swedish singer and the string players from Manchester apply themselves to music by a Tasmanian about the daily rites of Torres Strait Islanders. On our whirling globe with its transitory, jet-propelled people, isolation is no longer the demoralising fate it once was. Nor do we worry about upholding a narrow notion of Oz or Ockerland. A story in David Malouf's collection *Dream Stuff* reminds me of how shameful it used to be if you looked or sounded 'unAustralian', even for a moment. A little boy in Queensland loses his father during the war; his mother takes up with an American flyer, and some of this honorary uncle's mannerisms rub off on the kid. When he pronounces 'water' in the American way, flattening the a and thickening the t to a d, a playmate jeers 'Are you a Yank or something?' The boy flushes with shame: a 'defection from the local', as Malouf calls it, is tantamount to treason, nearly as bad as sounding like a Jap. Luckily we have outgrown this touchy xenophobia. But do we risk forfeiting the individuality that we nurtured for so long? The 'great world' which we have at last been invited to join has dispensed with roots and attachments; it discounts origins and disbelieves in originality, since everything is a facsimile of something else.

The presence of Fox Studios on the Sydney showgrounds announces the change. Here Australia used to parade its livestock and show off its agricultural produce; now, inside dark hangars, the farm is replaced by a factory of illusions. The Wachowski brothers inaugurated the place when they made *The Matrix*, set in a cybernetic future where our mental lives are controlled by software that drip-feeds us with lies. It's easy to spot Sydney in their film—the ziggurats of the financial district, the open-air food court of Australia Square, the back alleys of Glebe, and Chinatown near Darling Harbour, the vegetables on its market stalls juicily detonated by an exchange of gunfire during one of the chases. But the Wachowskis mystified the location by superimposing street names from their own native city, Chicago. The purpose was to suggest placelessness—a contemporary existential condition, inherent in a world where geographical distance has imploded. Thus Sydney's two unmistakable landmarks are kept hidden. The Opera House is never seen, and the Harbour Bridge is glimpsed only twice. One of its pylons skulks behind a skyscraper in the scene when the cybernetic agent played by Hugo Weaving interrogates Neo, and the entire spidery span is revealed for a moment in the final scene, as Neo makes a phone call from a cubicle in Martin Place. This game of hide and seek makes Sydney interchangeable with Chicago, Shanghai, or the rebuilt Berlin. Post-modern cities, in any case, are no more substantial than movie sets.

It's a contagious vision, and it can even overtake expatriates, who ought to know better. In 2000, after a decade in New York, Peter Carey returned to Sydney, intending—as he proprietorially put it—to 'make claim on the city'. The claim was imaginative, though he did cast an appraising eye on some real estate in Bondi. As his 747 swooped over the harbour, he craned to see the city framed in a porthole. He wanted to scale down Sydney to a single image, like an establishing shot in a film: the stern utilitarian bridge confronting the unfunctionally beautiful Opera House—a coathanger and a clump of shining, singing shells. But clouds effaced the view, and Carey made do with a video display on the monitor above his seat. Reality, described and photographed too often, expires in exhaustion; Sydney's best-known sights are victims of their own blatant, banal visibility. In his account of the visit, Carey excuses himself from mentioning the Harbour Bridge, which he has a phobia about: he once suffered a caffeine-induced panic attack while driving across it in peak hour. He glances at the Opera House from the Manly ferry, calls it 'a miracle', then summarises a lecture about it by a droning architectural engineer.

Oz

Sydney, competing with its image on so many glossy postcards, turns into a pallid copy of itself. The same thing happens to the bush, once the fortress that guarded Australia's uniqueness. A story by Frank Moorhouse describes a camping trip in the Great Dividing Range. Tramping through the undergrowth, the two walkers reach a lookout that looks out at nothing at all: European nature worship has been pointlessly mimicked here by the topographers of the Rotary Club. When they squat to cook dinner over a camp fire, the man doubts the woman's ability to cope. 'I came through the Australian experience too', she says indignantly, and he has to admit that she resembles someone 'out of the First Settlement'. But their regression is half-hearted. They treat themselves to a bottle of 1968 Coonawarra Cabernet Shiraz, unavailable to the pioneers. Later, as they plod through a swamp, he promises her a new pair of Keds. She doubts that he means it, and tells him, 'They come from the States.' Our intrepidity relies on imported footwear.

An American entrepreneur in Peter Carey's *Illywhacker* argues that Australia is a commercial property awaiting development. Carey himself believes that the geological shrines of the outback—Uluru, the Olgas—are mere sideshows, their mystique fabricated for the benefit of international tourists who won't want to linger in the thin coastal cities.

Countries these days see themselves as products, branded goods to be promoted around the world; the sales campaign inevitably traffics in lies. It's interesting that our global presence has been advanced by a series of actors, specialists in self-reinvention. Yet these performers, unlike Paul Hogan or Steve Irwin, don't deal in crass stereotypes. What they exemplify is our obliging adaptability. Hugh Jackman, in his first song in *The Boy from Oz*, makes this boast on behalf of the bisexual, bicoastal, bicontinental Peter Allen: he will transform himself into whatever you desire, or whatever the marketers decide they can sell. Is this what it means to be a boy or girl from Oz, in a borderless world where national identity is as obsolete as the nation state? Jackman's own repertoire extends from a sleek eighteenth-century British aristocrat to a hirsute wolfman. Russell Crowe can be a gladiator or a Princeton mathematician. Cate Blanchett is equally convincing as a Celtic fairy, a Tudor monarch, or an American frontier wife. Nicole Kidman assumes the identities and physiques of a harlot, a vampire, a robot, or an egg-headed White House aide with a special knowledge of nuclear smuggling. The only thing they're never required to be is themselves. If they wanted to play Australian characters, should they have stayed at home?

Of course not. Though the American casting agents may not realise it, the appeal of these people derives from quirky national characteristics that cannot be suppressed. There's a telling moment in Jane Campion's film of *The Portrait of a Lady*, when John Gielgud congratulates Kidman on receiving her first proposal of marriage. 'I told you you'd be a success over here,' he says. 'Americans are highly appreciated.' He's referring to her economic value: she is an heiress, whose fortune is coveted by impoverished European aristocrats. But what are Australians appreciated for? To begin with, for their unsocialised larrikinism. This is a quality flaunted by Mel Gibson as Mad Max or the madcap cop in *Lethal Weapon*. Crowe as Maximus knows that his murderous rampages in the Colosseum are entertaining. Americans—softer, more pampered, reluctant to be reckless and desperate to be liked—lack this antic danger. The female equivalent is a forthright intelligence, erotically thrilling despite its repudiation of glamour: the best example is Judy Davis, who in *Absolute Power* barks orders at a sadistic but weak-willed American President and his hulking security men. No American actress would have dared, as Davis recently did on television, to play Nancy Reagan as Lady Macbeth from Bel Air. Most highly appreciated, perhaps, is a certain candour, unspoiled but not uncritical, the result of a long time spent looking at the rest of the world from a quizzical distance without being looked at in return. My evidence is the first extended close-up of Kidman's face, as ingenuous as an opening flower, in *The Portrait of a Lady*. It is not the portrait of a nineteenth-century American lady but of a contemporary Australian woman.

In Patrick White's *The Solid Mandala*, the holy fool Arthur Brown ponders an image of totality. For him it is the sanctum housing a god: a speckled marble, with galactic whorls of light in its core. The 'perfect, glass sphere', which Arthur starrily gazes at, is for White the globe we inhabit, composed of two hemispheres. 'The world,' as Arthur wisely recognises, 'is another mandala'. The hemispheres are twins, like Arthur and his brother Waldo—inseparable, but for that reason fractious, mutually resentful, antagonistic. White's endeavour was to reunite the sundered halves, to recognise the complementarity of northern tragedy and southern comedy, Greece and Sarsparilla. Being Australian is enough to give you a headache: by sheer mental effort, you have to weld the world together. Or can we finally afford to relax? Perhaps the hemispheres no longer need us to splice or brace them.

Once there was a stark binary opposition between upper and lower. You made your choice, and—as I assumed when I left home at the age of twenty—it was irrevocable. But the mobile, malleable young Australians of today move back and forth between worlds I thought to be mutually exclusive, and they have more hemispheres than two to choose from. The children of my schoolfriends know about Hong Kong cinema, or take years off to work as language teachers in Japan. One of them—in her early twenties, with a law degree and a smooth fluency in European and Asian languages—manoeuvred the CEO of a Chinese airline in Beijing into parting with fees for the use of an Ansett flight simulator. She argued with him from a Melbourne office, speaking and writing immaculate Mandarin (with quotes every so often from Sun Tzu's *The Art of War*). Her opponent malingered for six months, then paid up when she threatened to arrest the next Chinese aircraft that touched down at Tullamarine. Jan Morris, mentally stripping the semi-marsupial mounted cops in the

Adelaide park, admired the beauty of this new breed. I tell the story about outwitting the Chinese to show that young Australians are just as impressive for their brains, which they exercise in a global arena.

Maps must be periodically redrawn, adjusted to our changed sense of Australia and its changing relations with the world. We are far from the superstitious ancient maps on which the southland's only purpose was to prop up the north; we are far too from the imperial maps sketched by Quirós and his colleagues, who searched the Pacific for replicas of Europe's religious and dynastic fiefdoms. In an earlier lecture I mentioned the map designed by Gert Sellheim in 1937, with its stormy dramatisation of a cultural showdown: a British galleon rams the western coast while the indigenous inhabitants gather in the east and prepare to flee. For Sellheim, the centre of Australia—the area over which those cultures quarrelled—remained unknown and unknowable.

On my wall in London I have a map that represents the way we think of Australia now. It's a bulging compendium assembled by the photographer Max Pam during 1999 and 2000 to celebrate Australia's autonomy and its confident rapprochement with the other continents. More than a map, it amasses snapshots, stamps, stencils, postal stickers, postcards, a page from a passport and the wrapping from a jar of Vegemite. Together with a smattering of smaller maps and state badges, these icons are arranged around the borders of a folded-out chart published by *National Geographic*.

Tales of Two Hemispheres

But Pam does not defer to American authority. In ink in the bottom left corner he corrects *National Geographic*'s version of Australia, pointing out that it gets the name of the Southern Ocean wrong. Opposing empires still encroach. The Australian postage stamps stuck to the margins carry portraits of British monarchs, and they are balanced—in one of the photographs collaged around the edge—by Mickey Mouse on the face of a watch. Our position remains precarious. On a meteorological diagram near the bottom right corner, trade winds bend and buckle Australia, which looks about to blow away.

A fringe of airmail stickers seems to be readying Pam's Australia for a trip overseas. In fact, the map commemorates the end of the photographer's early wanderings, after he returned from three years in Borneo. Red hand-marked lines strike out from the coast. At first sight they look like the yearning vectors of the shipping routes, along which Australians used to travel when they left home. Actually these are Pam's personal songlines. They point to hand-lettered reminiscences in the margins about his digressive rediscovery of the country, which took him from washing dishes in a Sydney hotel to membership of an Aboriginal community near Darwin.

Maps usually look down from a heady perch above the earth, but Pam's customised map charts terrain he has walked across or driven over. He writes on the land itself, as if making marks in the dust with a stick: hence the photograph of larvae inscribing their own testimony on the trunk of a scribbly gum.

Oz

This map is a personal reliquary and also what collectors used to call a 'Wunderkammer', storing souvenirs of fabled places encountered on the Grand Tour. Here we have Queensland's gigantic hollow pineapple, and a dairy cow whose interior you can also visit through a gaping door beneath its uplifted tail; I wish there had been room for the Big Merino in Goulburn, with its satanic horns and ghoulish green eyes. The postage stamps that form one of the borders take inventory of further marvels, actual and fictional. Uluru is included, asleep in a purple haze. So are the Three Sisters, those immobilised monoliths in the Blue Mountains that, like their namesakes in Chekhov's play, will probably never make it to Sydney. Another sticker shows Cradle Mountain in Tasmania, which does resemble the piece of nursery furniture it's named after. One stamp contains an image of a lion fish, heraldically striped; others commemorate Blinky Bill, the dozy koala, or Snugglepot and Cuddlepie the gum-nut babies—the playmates of my childhood.

Early map-makers indicated a border where knowledge gave way to strangeness, writing 'Here be dragons'. The red trails Pam inks in lead to anecdotes about watching raptors fly overhead in the Gulf of Carpentaria, swimming with deadly jellyfish, or wrestling a kangaroo that robbed a loaf of bread from his tent. But there is no zone where ignorance and fear take over. As he explains at the top and bottom of the map, he now lives on the coast outside Perth, with the Indian Ocean at his front door. He pities suburbanites who see only clothes lines

103

Tales of Two Hemispheres

and barbecue pits in the adjacent backyard and therefore 'miss the whole point of being located on the greatest of all islands'.

A beach like Pam's is the place we remember how we once gratefully clambered aboard this floating slab of land, like victims of a shipwreck. It is from here, too, that we contemplate our place in the world. Peter Sculthorpe's narrator sees the cliffs heaved from the ocean to announce the existence of the fifth and last continent. Rex Dupain ponders infinity at Bondi, and Percy Grainger studies tonal and metrical liberty by watching the waves at Brighton. Mad Max broods about the final showdown on the Mornington Peninsula, and the heroine of *On the Beach* drives out to the entrance of Port Phillip Bay to take her suicide pills, just as her American lover's submarine dives under. Robert Hughes, at the end of *The Fatal Shore*, crawls through bushes to the jagged rim of the Tasman Peninsula and gazes down on 'our imprisoning sea'. Are the oceans a perimeter fence of barbed wire? No, the view from the edge doesn't mean that we are castaways watching for a sail. By calling the continent an island, or 'the greatest of all islands', Pam declares that we have charted its margins, explored its interior, and can hold it all in our heads, as if Australia were the size of Tasmania.

To acknowledge the subjectivity of his map-making, Pam renames the continent. He labels it across the centre with two ripe, fruity, hand-painted letters: a succulent lime-green O and a lemon-yellow Z. Together they make the desert bloom. For once, the ideal place is not wishfully removed to the edge of possibility, or shunted out of sight around the corner of the globe. And, as I now realise with a twinge, you don't have to leave Oz to go back to dun-coloured, ordinary Kansas. Surrounded by a frieze of flying pineapples, this wonderland happens to be home.

appendices

The two essays that follow are revised versions of public lectures delivered in Hobart and Launceston in July 2004, as part of a series of events organised by the Tasmanian government to mark the bicentenary of the state. They were written at the same time as the Boyer Lectures, and deal with similar ideas in a more detailed and geographically concentrated way. I was honoured by the invitation from the late Jim Bacon, then Premier of Tasmania; I am grateful to Lynne Uptin for so skilfully organising my visit and for the warmth of her welcome.

1
'How to Like this Place'

Physical separateness means that Tasmania has always been self-aware. But that self-consciousness used to be defensive. During my boyhood, we looked towards the mainland with a mixture of intimidation and resentment. I remember my father telling me, after I described some tropical fruit I had eaten in Melbourne, that mangoes were banned in Tasmania. He approved of the prohibition; he always thought I had outlandish tastes, and couldn't see why I was not satisfied by apples. Today the barricades have been raised. You only need to stroll through the market on Salamanca Place in Hobart on Saturday morning and sample the produce to appreciate how much less stringently uniform the society is—no longer an outpost of wan, thin-blooded Anglo-Saxondom. These days you don't encounter embargoes telling you what it is proper to eat or think about, or who you are permitted to be.

There's a Chinese tailor around the corner from my apartment in New York who does expert alterations. In Greenwich

Village even the tailors are Confucian aphorists, so he advertises his skill with a sign in the window that says, 'If we weren't all different, how would we fall in love?' Because we differ from each other, we see the world differently, and art, like love, is the product of that difference. It's apt that the events celebrating the state's bicentenary have been collectively entitled 'Reflections of Tasmania'. Those reflections are plural, and probably contradictory. But the polite quarrel between them is enriching. Art multiplies reality; the mirror which does the reflecting is a magic one, because it changes what it reflects. Like the acts of those Aboriginal ancestors who fabricated the earth, art merges inner and outer, the mind and nature, and thereby makes us partners in the creative mystery that begot the lakes, the mountains, the men and the women. It is our wide-awake dreaming.

I grew up believing that art was something that had to be created elsewhere. In that elsewhere, Tasmania was a nowhere, noticed only if a joke was being made about it. Reading English books, I always watched out for references to Tasmania, which I hoped might validate my own existence: it didn't occur to me that I could do that for myself. But the odd acknowledgments I found were all snubs. A vulgar woman in Virginia Woolf's *Between the Acts* is rumoured to have 'been born, but it was only gossip said so, in Tasmania'. The rumour is a slur: her grandfather had been 'exported', and though her uncle was a bishop this merely goes to show that 'they forgot and forgave very easily in the Colonies'.

'How to Like this Place'

Noël Coward in *Private Lives* has a character remark, 'I once had an Aunt who went to Tasmania'. The line is as lethal as an execution, meant to provoke automatic laughter, and when I see the play I still flush with indignation while everyone else titters. The polyglot puns in Joyce's *Finnegans Wake* smudge the state's name into 'Tossmania', which—because 'tosse' in Portuguese means cough—is said to be a nasty winter ailment. We were either rendered unmentionable or, if you imagine that maniacal coughing fit, reduced to an impolite spluttering noise.

These slights worried me for a long while. Thanks to Yahoo Serious, I no longer waste time brooding over them. In *Young Einstein*, the comedian with the electrified ginger hair splits a beer atom in rural Tasmania to carbonate the local brew, and in the process happens upon the secret of nuclear fission. He goes on to invent the electric guitar, rock and roll, and the surfboard. These later achievements happen on the mainland, but he eats Tasmanian apples to feed his brain, so we can claim some of the credit. The film is a serious joke: why shouldn't our state produce a great artist or scientist? Marginalised on islands of their own, the English and Irish insisted on their centrality. For each of us as individuals, the centre of the world is wherever we happen to be born.

The humanistic idea of art arrived here from Europe very early, but it only served to vex and demean the colonists it was meant to benefit. In 1833 Benjamin Duterrau, who painted George Augustus Robinson's attempted reconciliation with the

Aboriginal people, gave a lecture to the Mechanics' Institute in Hobart on Raphael's 'School of Athens'. It was probably the first such evangelising occasion in any of the Australian colonies, but it was as wrong-headed as Robinson's noble folly. Raphael's painting in the papal library at the Vatican organises classical culture into a serene conversation between art and science. The ancients and the moderns confer in a vaulted forum under the auspices of Apollo, who strums the lyre which signifies art's elucidation of the refractory world. I wonder what the artisans of Hobart felt about Duterrau's account of the work. I suspect they were crushed by it. The lecture assumed that art's function was to construct a whitely Platonic citadel. Plato in Raphael's painting points upwards, indicating the sky: art supposedly ensures man's ascent to heaven, or to the immaterial kingdom of the ideal. For local purposes, he should have been pointing in the opposite direction. Art needs to be homegrown. But how—in the inhospitable, bloodsoaked penal outpost—could it dig beneath Raphael's geometrical pavement and root itself in native ground?

Apollo did not take up residence in Tasmania, even though Lady Jane Franklin built him a little temple in the suburban backwoods of Lenah Valley. In Hal Porter's *The Tilted Cross*, this stainless heritage is assaulted by savage, disruptive energies that cannot be soothed by Apollo's music: Hobart's weather, Porter says, is 'gothic', not balmily Grecian. The Hobart of Porter's novel is a chilly inferno, a Hades in which the golden artist Judas

'How to Like this Place'

Griffin Vaneleigh (based on transported painter Thomas Griffiths Wainewright) is trapped and destroyed, as if the sun itself had been quenched. The town's very topography supplied Porter with a map of this underworld: the rivulet, thick with muck and offal, belches beneath a bridge in Campbell Street ironically named after the neoclassical architect Palladio. More recently, Lady Franklin's decrepit and deconsecrated temple reappears in Louis Nowra's play *The Golden Age*. Here it is used as a backdrop for a performance of Euripides' tragedy about Iphigenia, the priestess who is required to sacrifice her brother Orestes. At least the tragedy with its brutal rites admits the barbarity of the Greeks, which connects them to what Nowra calls the 'human barbarism' of Van Diemen's Land, where the horizontal forest of the west coast entombs a lost tribe of genetic throwbacks.

The august standards invoked by Duterrau were demeaning and disabling. It took courage to acclimatise the classics, and to cast off the bitter irony of Porter or Nowra. But why shouldn't literature begin its history all over again in Tasmania, starting from the rural routines commemorated by Hesiod or Theocritus? In her 'Oyster Cove Pastorals', Gwen Harwood calls the roll of her chooks, which are named after Homeric warriors—Hector, Achilles, Ajax—and notes admiringly that their plumes are gilded by Helios, the sun-god Apollo, who also shines on us. In another poem, Harwood summons Mnemosyne, the mother of all the Greek muses, and instructs her to commemorate local experience:

> Sing, memory, sing those seasons in the freezing
> suburb of Fern Tree, a rock-shaded place
> with tree ferns, gullies, snowfalls and eye-pleasing
> prospects from paths along the mountain-face.

Harwood assumes that, for the goddess, Mount Wellington and Mount Olympus are interchangeable. Although she calls on Mnemosyne to help, the achievement of humanising nature and uplifting fallen Tasmania is hers alone. At the end of a poem which recalls how she gave birth to her children and nursed them at Fern Tree, she even turns Mount Wellington from a stern male presence to a soft, wet, nurturing female force, a Magna Mater. She and a friend climb towards the summit 'like gods or blessed spirits', and look down from

> above the leafy dazzle of the streams
> to fractured rock, where water had its birth,
> and stood in silence, at the roots of dreams,
> content to know: our children walk the earth.

Those children are one aspect of Harwood's posterity; her poems are another, perhaps even more precious because they reveal how you can love a place as fiercely as you might love a person.

Love of country—not patriotism but the tender incorporation in a personal landscape—ought be instinctive, the very basis of our humanity. But in Tasmania, because of the state's early history, that love had to learned. James McAuley in 'Autumn in

Hobart', a brief and quietly mournful poem written near the end of his life, notices the city's showery weather and takes dictation from a lyricist who celebrates it:

> The yellow-throated honeyeater knows
> How to like this place.

The bird is a reproof to those, like me, who didn't possess that knowledge and had difficulty acquiring it. Yet how could I share that intimate affinity when literature, an art so much more querulous than the bird's wordless music, had alienated me from the place and the spirits living in it? Wrongly, I thought of culture as the antithesis of nature. I therefore placed myself apart from or outside the community to which the honeyeater unquestioningly belonged.

Still, I insist on blaming others for my estrangement. Early descriptions of the island scourged it with metaphors; its very creation, as registered by literature, was a destructive act. Marcus Clarke in *For the Term of His Natural Life* treats the waves of Bass Strait as carnivores or cannibals which have 'bitten a mouthful out … Victoria', and compares the south-east coast of Tasmania to 'a biscuit at which rats have been nibbling'. The creator of this place is a blundering ogre, scattering fragments of land like 'the curious forms assumed by melted lead spilt into water', fashioning deformations like the place named Three Thumbs, just off Maria Island on the west coast. Growing up, you need reassurance, and can expect to be told that you're beautiful because—to those who love you—you truly are. How damaging it is to be taught that you live in a place whose landscape is disfigured, abortive. Yet this is the view Marcus Clarke takes of Tasmania's irregular coast. Safely entering the channel, he sights the projection of Bruny Island, which he compliments as 'the Italy of this miniature Adriatic'—but the image is hardly Arcadian, because once more it is twisted painfully awry: 'the Italian boot' has 'its toe bent upwards'. Our geography is schizoid. Though Clarke concedes that the Derwent Valley smiles, on the west coast 'the face of nature is stamped with a perpetual frown'. The grimace, of course, is on the face of the writer himself.

A rhetorical tradition emerges from these descriptions, which I can only classify as geographical scatology. Hal Porter for instance sees Van Diemen's Land as an 'ugly trinket suspended at the world's discredited rump'; he was probably thinking of those dried faeces trapped on the woolly rump of a sheep, and the cloacal image confirms that Hobart originally served as 'the privy of London'. Robert Hughes too is enthusiastically insanitary in *The Fatal Shore*, using his painterly eye to define the peat-stained water of Macquarie Harbour as a 'urinous froth'. The words of Porter or Hughes look obscene on the page, but you sense a certain gusto behind them: a delight in depicting the unmentionable, a verbal fury that rises up against the distant standards of English literary gentility. Even Richard Flanagan allows his hero in *Death of a River Guide* to view Strahan as 'a crusty skin cancer on the flesh of south-west Tasmanian wilderness'. But there is a tough love in such images. Lesions are growths, organic offshoots of the body they feed on; the crust, like a scab, might be protecting the raw flesh beneath it, covering it while it heals. This was always a hard place, and the affection it excites is gruff, grizzled, camouflaged—in a way that is inimitably Australian—as matey disparagement.

My own youthful obsession with English literature meant that I could only ever see Tasmania obliquely. I was living in what McAuley once called a 'land of similes', and that double vision made the reality swim out of focus. I well remember, when I was writing my book about Tasmania, that my friend Iris Murdoch advised against its title, *Down Home*—a phrase of my mother's, referring to the orchard in the Huon Valley where she grew up. 'You should call it *Prospero's Island*,' Iris decreed. But the island which is Prospero's autocratic domain in *The Tempest* is a place of disgruntled exile; his home is in Milan, and he returns to it at the end of the play. Although I kept my own title, I wasn't entirely able to see around or through such literary impositions. After all, I inherited a convention of misunderstanding that went back as far as the first explorers. Quirós wanted to find similitudes of the northern hemisphere down in these latitudes, because he hoped to prove God's omnipresence. Other navigators used similes that were scenic rather than spiritual, but they too wished to reduce a new world to familiarity. John Campbell, who anthologised the reports of the explorers in 1744, concluded from his reading of Tasman's voyage that Van Diemen's Land was 'in all respects' a facsimile of the south of France. Well, Hobart today may be chic, but it's still not much like Cannes. Why can't it be unique, resembling only itself?

Metaphor has a wanderlust fidgeting within it. The word metaphor refers to the process of carrying or transporting; a metaphor is a figure of speech with wings, and it sets out to effect a metamorphosis as it flies through space to turn one thing into another that may be quite unlike it. Hence the aerial bridges between hemispheres constructed by Tasmanian writers. Hal Porter claimed that Hobart, spilling down the mountainside towards the waterfront, resembled Naples, Genoa or perhaps San Francisco. A character in *Death of a River Guide* muses on a postcard of Trieste: 'with its houses clustering on hills, and its harbour, it looked a bit like Hobart'. None of these likenesses makes sense to me, though I'm not immune to the habit of imagining a reunion of the sundered hemispheres. I once spent an afternoon in a garden north of Copenhagen, looking over the empty sound towards the low yellow hills of Sweden. I wondered after a while why I felt so happy, so pacified, and realised that it was because the colours of the land, the bright clean air and the glassy water, reminded me of the view from Hobart across the harbour to the eastern shore.

Settlers found a protective magic in such analogies, choosing place names so as to connect the obdurate facts of Tasmania with fictional prototypes at home. The ticket-of-leave man John Mitchel wanted to 'berhyme' Lake Sorell, which deserved the same literary honours as Windermere, Loch Lomond or Killarney; that rhyming motive inscribed itself across the map of Tasmania, placing the Vale of Rasselas just behind Maydena, and commemorating a feudal character from Walter Scott's *The Lay of the Last Minstrel* at Deloraine on the north-west coast. English literary visitors colonised Tasmania by cataloguing supposed affinities. The mail coaches with liveried drivers convinced Anthony Trollope that 'everything in Tasmania is more English than in England itself': a sarcastic remark, which suggests that the colony is a little too earnest in its mimicry. In 1940 Arnold Haskell annexed Tasmania all over again, and used it in order to smugly dismiss the mainland: 'The Englishman, who understands islands, and who often reacts violently against the immensity of Australia, will love Tasmania … He will find it somewhere not very far from Scotland.' The truth of course is that it could hardly be further from Scotland.

These stretched connections distorted the sight-lines of those who grew up here and, knowing no better, took the similes on trust. Christopher Koch remembers sailing across to Maria Island with Vivian Smith. The young writers, observing the frigid sea and the bleak light and looking towards the overgrown ruins on the shore, 'imagined the scene to be like the Hebrides—although neither of us had ever been to Scotland'. They laughed at the way they had been duped by a literary fantasy. Our coasts offered Koch a succession of beguiling prospects, though what he and his characters saw was always an alternative to Tasmania. The narrator in his novel *The Doubleman* admires the Hazards, and thinks that these 'lavender peaks' resemble 'South Sea islands, beyond the sun's glittering track'. Tasmania is a miniaturised globe—Hebridean at one moment, Polynesian at the next.

Let me tell you a story to illustrate what it was like to live in that looking-glass world, where the reflections of Tasmania were actually derivative pictures of inaccessible places half a world away. For a while during 1962 I was let off school to appear in a film of Nan Chauncy's *They Found a Cave*. I played one of a tribe of English evacuees, displaced persons befriended by a local lad whose name, just to enforce his indigenous status, was Tas; I didn't have to ape a British accent because my voice was dubbed by a plummy middle-aged lady. The only good thing about the film is Peter Sculthorpe's score, performed on the harmonica by Larry Adler. A little waltz has stayed with me ever since, and it catches the mood of my adolescence and of Tasmania in those days: it is chirpy yet somehow bereft, wheeling round in circles until, like a tired child, it runs out of energy and sags into depression. Not long ago, I was disconcerted to find out that the tune has nothing at all to do with Tasmania, or with Nan Chauncy's cave-dwellers. Its proper title is *Left Bank Waltz*, and Sculthorpe wrote it in 1958 to evoke the breezy, free-wheeling atmosphere of the Latin Quarter. Music that for me sounded bucolic and Tasmanian was actually urbane and Parisian, its brittle vivacity lapsing into existential gloom. But the story is even stranger, because Sculthorpe too—

though older than me and already well-travelled—lived in our world of cheating mirrors. When he wrote the waltz, he had never been on the Left Bank of the Seine. He had only glimpsed the wet, bleary Parisian suburbs as he passed through on a train to London from Genoa, where he disembarked from the liner that had brought him from Australia. I wonder whether he thought that Genoa was like Hobart?

Although Sculthorpe has spent his life elsewhere, I am sure that one source of his music—along with influences from Arnhem Land and Asia—is Tasmania and its native sounds. A phrase in his autobiography is potent enough to make my throat tighten: he describes 'the wind singing in the sky, just as it did in Tasmania'. When I read that, I can hear it too. I locate the noise in Castle Forbes Bay beside the Huon River, where during my own childhood I used to hear the trees on the steep hills above my grandfather's orchard sighing or moaning as the wind lashed them. Sculthorpe was lucky enough to hear a song; I, with my different temperament, heard something more like a howl. The sound made him a musician, since music traps and regulates such breezes; it made me want to use words, which were my own way of translating feeling into thought, of making the noise articulate. There's an extra irony in the fact that Sculthorpe overheard the echo of that gale during the 1970s in Sussex, where the rolling hills, the oaks, elms and 'the inevitable old stone church' all recalled Tasmania. Artists are congenitally discontented. At home, we crave a sight of places that are different and distant, where we can reinvent ourselves. Having got there, we find we are suffering from homesickness.

This colonial pining for a world elsewhere may sound now like idle daydreaming, but it could turn nasty. Told that your surroundings are inferior, you punish them for it. Louisa Ann Meredith, describing 'the improvement and civilisation' of her home at Swansea during the 1850s, instigates a genteel vendetta against the local trees, which are only tolerable when cut down to be planed and polished into furniture. Helped along by the axe and the lathe, ironbarks and stringybarks, she says, acquire 'some resemblance to oak'. Clearing the ground around her house, Mrs Meredith is prepared to spare a lightwood tree, redeemed by its yellow flowers and their 'hawthorn scent'. But the terms in which she describes her clemency are sinister: 'One singularly handsome tree of this kind we marked for preservation, amidst the doomed throng of less eligible residents on the piece of scrub and forest destined to become our garden.' The doomed throng of ineligible residents is human as well as arboreal; she describes a genocide practised by governments as well as gardeners, and declares this to be a work justified by destiny. The eucalypts are being ethnically cleansed, uprooted and executed.

Romanticism, which the colonists brought here with them, professed a religious reverence for nature. At the same time it relished scenarios of destruction like the one Mrs Meredith describes. Sublimity challenged men to do psychological battle with nature, whose marauding energies threatened to annihilate us. Wordsworth in *The Prelude* said that the debris left behind by an avalanche in the Swiss Alps looked apocalyptic, and Byron at the end of *Childe Harold's Pilgrimage* invited the ocean to roll over the populated continents and consume them. They delighted in the prospect of extinction: the nearer they got to the maelstrom, the more valiant they felt. Amanda Lohrey detected that romantic frisson during the Tasmanian bushfires of 1967, with their 'glowing beauty' and 'thrilling apocalyptic flare'. As the flames reduce the outer suburbs of Hobart to cinders, the homeowners in her novel *The Reading Group* feel an illicit excitement: 'Awe. It was a quality missing from their lives.' Awe is the appropriate response to the presence of a god, who on that terrible day became incarnate as fire. No wonder Richard Flanagan blames the imported cult of romantic sublimity for the dams that redesigned the landscape of the Tasmanian highlands. The energies of nature—its wild rivers and rearing, convulsive mountains—make god terrifyingly manifest. Man retaliates by deploying his own god-like machinery, and triumphs over turbulent water and obstructive rock.

Told that we were accursed, we sought absolution. A smug pastor in Flanagan's novel *Gould's Book of Fish* praises the convict artist because his paintings reveal 'the hope of Divine Redemption through Nature, which is Art'. Place-names in the highlands—settlements like Paradise and Promised Land, or the scriptural narrative written on stone in the Walls of Jerusalem—expressed the same allegorical hope. But in

Tales of Two Hemispheres

Tasmania, art that did the redeeming on its own, not in the name of a divinity who sanctified the cruelty of the penal system and blessed genocide. Writers wittily picked at flaws in Christianity's casual arrogation of this new terrain. Hal Porter noticed that the Southern Cross is tilted, and Helen Hodgman's narrator in *Blue Skies* candidly admits that she can't tell exactly where the cruciform pattern of stars is supposed to be: 'fortunately it's on the flag'.

The writer in Vivian Smith's poem 'The Colonial Poet', amazed by fern fronds and trying not to liken them to bishops' croziers, acknowledges the inspiration of Flanagan's convict artist: he wants 'to make each stanza look as if/ it had been drawn by Gould'. The redeemer here is Gould, whose painted fish re-create a creation not described in Genesis. Flanagan's Gould knows that he is 'singing a new genesis'. In my own book, I couldn't help being snide about the township of Paradise, since I situated Tasmania east of Eden; Flanagan in *Death of a River Guide*, to my astonishment, shows that it deserves the name by making it the location for a visionary marvel. The narrator looks down 'the road from Paradise, on the way to Beulah', which is a Blakean condition of wedded bliss; he sees there a clump of 'silver- and salmon-trunked stringybarks', beneath one of which a dead child is buried. Made sacred by this grave, the tree is now 'the flowering gum of Paradise', and it defies the dull norms of nature by blossoming in winter. Later it lifts off and fires itself into the sky. Art has its

'How to Like this Place'

own white magic, challenging the black magic of those early descriptions of Tasmania as Hades.

Gould, in Flanagan's novel, confesses that he has 'stolen songs from God'. The self-accusation is unnecessary: the God served by the hypocrites who built the chapel at Port Arthur had no desire to sing Tasmania into being. According to the first geographical moralists, the deity defaced it or left it half-created, as Rowcroft's farmer contends in *Tales of the Colonies*. (He adds that the fumbling mistakes made down here were corrected when the time came to fashion the northern continents). But art knows how to hallow a place that God apparently deprecated. In 'View from the Domain', Smith notices Hobart's plentiful supply of churches: 'every inner hill contains a steeple'. His own 'holy places', however, are more innocuous, private or even secret, not marked by spires but consecrated by childhood memories. His old school (mine too) with its 'fading pink cement' is one of these; there are also the plane trees in a park he doesn't need to name because it is obviously Franklin Square. In a poem about returning to Hobart from Sydney, Smith anchors himself again in the home he left with a sideways glance from the taxi. 'A gull stands on one leg in Fitzroy Place,' he says; like a magic spell or a photograph, that line freezes a moment and makes it eternal. For me, when I read it recently in London, it did something else. It made me see Fitzroy Place, and made me feel that I too, like the gull, was standing there. The same poem finds a revelation in the 'lunar vacancy' of Hobart on a Sunday, as Smith arrives at the empty airways office and sees 'shop windows like aquariums of clouds'. Poetic insight brings the sky down to earth, and atones for what I remember as the dreariness of those deserted streets on days when the shops were closed.

The miracle can be made to happen by the simplest of poetic acts—by uttering a name and giving it a liquid, lilting musicality. There's a poem by Gwen Harwood about a colonial graveyard that begins, simply and movingly, with the word 'Tasmania'. This is not the title but the first word of the poem itself, and you feel the pleasure she takes in metrically inflecting it, savouring it in silence, then writing it down. After describing the refreshed spring weather, she remembers the unresurrected dead beneath the ground; the poem goes on to convert grief into a joy as bright and warming as the season. Another poem of hers achieves a different sanctification in its description of September snow. A blizzard in the city honours the imperial potentates in Franklin Square,

> ... piling ermine on
> King Edward's mantle, covering Sir John
> Franklin's heroic seagull-favoured head.

Nature improves the monarch's regalia, and even birdshit becomes a blessing. Bad weather brings out the best in Tasmanian writers: Flanagan's Gould watches snow soothe Hobart, and sees the flakes 'like lost dreams ... waltzing through [a] hushed world'. After this bleached purification, a

'How to Like this Place'

poem by Harwood about spring at Oyster Cove, dedicated to the memory of James McAuley, is dazzled and comforted by the colour that sparkles on the water or seeps from the earth:

> Sapphire, turquoise, pastoral
> viridian on the hills of Bruny.

With characteristic daring, Harwood alters one of Shakespeare's best-known lines when she says of her purged September vista, 'Whiteness is all.' In a poem describing autumn in the Huon Valley, McAuley comes teasingly close to paraphrasing Shakespeare's original praise of ripeness. The boughs sag almost pregnantly with the weight of their apples, 'pears ripen yellow', Keatsian juices ooze. A moral tag is attached to the view, as if this were an illustration in a medieval Book of Hours, but the last lines simply listen to the sound of the harvest:

> Life is full of returns;
> It isn't true that one never
> Profits, never learns:
>
> Something is gathered in,
> Worth the lifting and stacking;
> Apples roll through the graders,
> The sheds are noisy with packing.

I admire the way that McAuley finds a consolatory meaning in the seasonal, cyclical recurrences of nature. But what I love about the poem is the way it evokes the creak of the grader's rolling belt as it trundled the apples along in the packing shed on my grandfather's orchard. It fixes in words my fugitive memories; once again, it gives me my childhood back, and convinces me that I never lost it. Like apples wrapped in twists of white paper and carefully positioned in crates, poems package emotions and send them off to be consumed by others. The words trigger feelings that sustain us, like food or like heat.

There's an additional example in a poem by Smith called 'Warmth in July: Hobart', where the brief efflorescence of winter light is a token of nature's eventual reawakening and a symptom of the affection that poetry seeks to disseminate. While the sun gilds the air and takes the chill off it, Smith instructs the reader to 'feel the light' and suggests that, if we do so, we will have begun to appreciate the way art transforms sensation into understanding:

> ... all your knowledge is mere warmth and glow,
> all apprehension—as of sensual ease:
> a sense of sure precision deep in things.

As with 'Whiteness is all', I cherish these occasions when our writers echo English literary predecessors or (even better) raise their voices to out-talk them. Here Smith is almost paraphrasing Wordsworth, whose poetry attempts to 'see into the life of things'. But despite this philosophical ambition, he thinks of art's task in a homespun way that is endearingly Tasmanian.

Warmth is important in our cold climate. In one poem Smith says that the foothills of Mount Wellington, painted by colonial artists, look 'woollen', which makes them furry protectors. In another, succinctly entitled 'Tasmania', he says that the hills 'rot like rugs', as if they were carpet exposed outdoors. The same fond perception makes Flanagan's Gould say that 'snow mantled the mountain' while mist covers Hobart 'like a slow-falling quilt'. The earth is our garment, or a precious insulation; even snow is an eiderdown, contriving to keep the cold out. Poetry can be a source of radiant comfort, like a hearth.

Words have the magical capacity to accomplish this transformation, but the art of McAuley's honeyeater—tactfully wordless because it bypasses the reason—is even more effective. Of course it's one thing to transform snowflakes into a feather bed and something else to look for redemptive reassurance after the deaths of thirty-six innocent people. Still, music helped Tasmania adjust to an intolerable reality in 1996 when, two months after the shootings at Port Arthur, Peter Sculthorpe's brief elegy for the victims and the survivors was performed at Government House. *Port Arthur: In Memoriam* knows better than to risk grand tragic rhetoric, because the composer doesn't presume to intrude on a private grief or pretend that he can feel its intensity. For three minutes Sculthorpe's orchestra ponders the event, quietly and hesitantly as if stunned by incomprehension. The rhythm is a gentle rocking, which makes you feel that you are held in arms that cradle and calm you; a lamenting trumpet plays a reveille, ensuring that we do not forget. Twice, the solemnity is interrupted by a stabbing shock. The rhythm falters, the strings expose a raw, fragile vulnerability for a few bars, then the trumpet recovers its composure and continues the ceremony. The two interruptions are a reminder that art is powerless to prevent such outrages—though the second is less disabling than the first, so time, which music seeks to organise, has perhaps already begun the work of healing. It's a modest piece, but *Port Arthur: In Memoriam* demonstrates how important it is for a society to reflect on itself by making art.

The world at large overlooks Tasmania, which ought not to matter to us. In England most people think it's an independent country, or else part of New Zealand. Americans have no idea at all who or where we are: I have met people who assume I come from Tanzania. Hiding at the bottom of the map, we occupy a speck of space that is at least instantly recognisable. The island's shape makes it iconic, though the iconography hasn't always been flattering. Those who are kindly disposed towards us might say that Tasmania is heart-shaped, or—like Christopher Koch—see it 'hanging like a shield above Antarctica'. But other metaphors deface and injure Tasmania: Hal Porter thought that it resembled 'a much-kicked bucket', which makes it synonymous with death. The image I like best is more lyrical, entrancing even if improbable. In the 1880s Jessie Couvreur said that Tasmania, 'with its encircling chains of mountains, folded one around the other, … was like a mighty rose, tossed from the Creator's hand into the desolate Southern Ocean'. It worries me that the creator, once more disowning us, has negligently tossed the flower away. But at least the rose is 'mighty', and the verbal sorcery I treasure is present in the way mountains are transmuted into clustered petals. Jessie Couvreur loved Tasmania so much that she rechristened herself after it, and adopted the pen-name Tasma.

My mistake, and that of the culture I grew up in, was to assume that the world lay offshore, beginning perhaps with those misty vistas—reminiscent both of Scotland and Hawaii—that Koch thought he saw just off the east coast. You become a grown-up when you stop comparing yourself with others—either wanting to be them, or belittling them because they are not you—and begin to accept and prize your idiosyncrasy. Having done so, you then gain access to the singular, incomparable universe inside yourself, with all its intriguing complications, its quirks and proud peculiarities. John Donne declared in a sermon that no man was an island, which could not be less true. We are all islands; insularity is a condition of our being, and something we should cherish.

In *The Boys in the Island*, Koch defines Tasmania as 'a land outside history, almost outside time'. A different and more literally wholesome faith is propounded in Flanagan's *Death of a River Guide*: the Franklin River is 'a world pure and whole and complete unto itself', and—later—one of its gorges is 'a world complete unto itself'. The repeated 'unto itself' has a biblical intonation, since ecology looks at nature with a religious fervour. Elsewhere in the novel, Tasmania is defined as 'a world total and full in itself'. I am tempted to twist the phrase and point out that Flanagan is likening Tasmania to an egg: it is, as we used to say, as full as a goog. And in fact this is exactly the analogy he intends, though without any implication of drunkenness. The narrator of the novel is born inside a caul, a 'translucent egg'. He emerges into the daylight 'still enclosed in that elastic globe of life'. When cut out, he retains a longing for that amniotic ocean, and he merges with it once more when he drowns. That is the chosen fate for Flanagan's heroes, though it is hardly fatal: Gould dives into the harbour, grows gills, becomes one of his own fish, and ends in an aquarium. Tasmania is small enough to be a womb, but also immense enough to be a brain, because it encompasses the far-flung spaces we travel around when thinking. A piner rowing his punt from Strahan on the west coast towards the wild rivers has a mind—as Flanagan wonderingly puts it—'as empty and as vast and as still as the inland sea called Macquarie Harbour'. This revelation of Tasmania's self-sufficiency resounds like a contemporary anthem. It turns up again in the text of a talk by the architect Robert Morris-Nunn at a conference in Hobart in 1994. Morris-Nunn said that he hoped the Visitors' Centre he designed at Strahan—a hut for a post-modern piner—would show those who went there that 'Tasmania is not some hick backwater, but rather a world rich and powerful beyond even their dreaming'. I think you can hear Flanagan whispering in

'How to Like this Place'

Morris-Nunn's ear; 'rich and powerful' hints at the 'rich and strange' surrealism of Prospero's island, though the dream built on the west coast prefers to invoke the myth-making creativity of Aboriginal dreaming.

Death of a River Guide sums up the colonial century that preceded this current surge of artistic life: 'Nobody spoke. Unless it was to lie, nobody spoke.' Those who wanted to write ran away to do so, though as they abscond they are chased by an accusation, so baleful that Flanagan prints it in loud italics: '*If you leave you can never be free.*' On behalf of the accused, let me conclude by responding to that. I did leave in quest of freedom, and I think I found it, so I'm not inclined to accept the truth of the charge. But once you realise that you cannot free yourself, you are free to recognise that you don't want to.

Freedom need not entail denial. Wherever I live, I recreate Tasmania around myself. My garden in London has a tiny abbreviated gully of tree ferns, which I planted because they remind me of the humid, matted lower slopes of Mount Wellington. An urban fox chews the sprinklers that keep their furry trunks wet, so I even have a slightly mangy substitute for a Tasmanian devil. Upstairs in my bedroom, there is a shrine that enables me to pretend that the walls are transparent—a series of golden-toned nineteenth-century photographic panoramas of Mount Wellington and the harbour; another photograph of the mountain after a snowfall by Jack Cato, a Tasmanian lad who became Melba's protégé; and an ink drawing of Hobart made in

Tales of Two Hemispheres

1936 by Robert Emerson Curtis, which assembles a lucky dip of local symbols—double-decker buses, the funnels of the apple boats, the glaring sign of Tattersalls Club, cans of IXL jam and a catch of crayfish—and holds them together in a fishnet. In another corner there are some framed labels from apple crates that Nigel Triffit gave me once in Melbourne, with polished red fruit hanging in the sky above a purple Mount Wellington, and a dry-point etching presented to me by Geoff Dyer during a visit to London, a densely cross-hatched, tangled image of Roaring Meg, a waterfall outside Queenstown on the west coast.

As if these genii of place were not enough, on my bed I have the ultimate security blanket: a sheepskin rug, so big that an entire flock must have donated fleece for it, which I bought in one of the shops near Parliament House the last time I was in Hobart. It looks like the snowy comforter that Gould sees draped over the town, though it's actually as heavy as an avalanche. I have to say that it contributes more to my sense of safety than the burglar alarm or the panic buttons scattered around the house. At night I wriggle under it, and if I'm lucky I dream of Tasmania.

2
Thirty-six Views of Mount Wellington

Mountains turn the grounded men who live beneath them into metaphysicians. Take the case of Mount Wellington, which frowns down on Hobart like a moody, domineering god. Its concussed brow catches the sun as it rises, though every dawn is different: sometimes flushed and crimson, sometimes gold, occasionally misty and mysterious. You seem, as you stare up at it, to be watching lighting rehearsals for the first day of creation. And although you are only four thousand feet below, you might be foundering in some abysmal depth as you try to account for it. The conundrum has less to do with space than with time. The black peak with its strewn boulders was once a beach—the furthest limit of land, abruptly jutting into the water like a diving board. Hobart sits on what used to be the sunken ocean floor. Mount Wellington, despite its adamantine bulk, is a reminder that the earth only pretends to be fixed and solid. Its ridges and escarpments were forced from the ground by those tectonic shifts that have left fissures, like recent surgical scars, across the landscape of the Tasmanian south-west.

The mountain remains unstable, dangerously whimsical. It comes and goes on winter days, disappearing to reconsider its position and then, when the snowstorms pass, shedding its veils as if to make manifest some power that lies behind nature, beyond sight. Growing up in the northern suburbs of Hobart beneath one of its flanks, I always thought of it as a sleeping beast, a totemic animal that we needed to placate. The Aboriginal people, who called it Kunanyi, viewed it with the same superstitious reverence. Religions have placed various markers on Mount Wellington. By seeing the pillars of rock near the peak as organ pipes, Christianity made the mountain into a church, dedicated to an Anglican God who was converting a new hemisphere. But the proprietors of an English tea room that used to exist just off Strickland Avenue prayed to another deity: in their garden, which merged with the foothills, they placed an outsize statue of the Buddha.

The first contingents of penal administrators, however, saw nothing up there but an outsize piece of furniture: they bluntly squared and bevelled it by naming it Table Mountain. Could you really entrust a tea tray to this volcanic headland, made of rock that still looks molten and has an immobilised wave cresting at its summit? After the Peninsular War and the final victory against Napoleon, the colonists had the chance to ennoble the mountain, so they renamed it after a British military commander who never set eyes on it.

The mountain puzzled theologians and vexed the officials who handed out names to colonial places, but it was a gift to artists. The convict painter Thomas Watling complained that Australia was hopelessly unpicturesque because it lacked a horizon. How could an artist cope with space unless he had 'bold rising hills' to close off the visual field or 'azure distances' to soften the vanishing point? Mount Wellington made up for both deficiencies. Somewhere on its lower slopes there is a gully called Salvator Rosa Glen, named by an early aesthete who saw Mount Wellington romantically. Salvator was a baroque painter based in Naples during the seventeenth century, celebrated for his shaggy, jagged, brigand-infested Calabrian landscapes; Hazlitt thought he could see the imprint of Pan's hoof on his paintings, as if the goat-god, the spirit of nature's wildness, had helped produce them. Giving Salvator a cosy Hebridean glen on the mountain was a way of summoning art to take up residence here.

When the American painter Thomas Cole set out to explore the Hudson River Valley in 1835, he rejoiced to see mountains 'never beheld by Claude or Salvator'. But Van Diemen's Land wanted to behold itself through the eyes of Claude Lorraine or Salvator, and relied on pictorial protoypes to compose vistas of neoclassical serenity or romantic sublimity. Also during the 1830s, John Glover nicknamed areas on his property in the Tasmanian midlands Painter's Vale or Painter's Plains, since nature there had compliantly composed itself into the kind of view Glover had already studied in the Roman Campagna. It was a blinkered vision, but it persisted for a long while. In a poem about the protests in the 1970s against the flooding of the Franklin River, Vicki Raymond remembers the habit of looking at picturesque scenery reflected in the curved, gilded mirror of a Claude glass, and links this 'curious fashion' with the blindness of the politicians who dismissed the river as a leech-infested ditch.

Cole declared that 'the painter of American scenery has ... privileges superior to any other. All nature here is new to art'. That pride in the new land's novelty and superiority derived from the heady experience of national liberation. Colonised Australians were content to imagine how the country might look if some god-like foreign artist were to grace it with a visit and beatify it in paint. That's still true for Robert Hughes, who can only describe Norfolk Island by saying that 'the mornings are by Turner, the evenings by Caspar David Friedrich'. Though that takes care of events in the sky, a third artist has to be imported to cope with the island's vegetation: Hughes likens the bent, clawing bushes on the cliffs to 'Hokusai's "Great Wave" copied by a topiarist'. Seen in this way, our nature was not new to art. Instead, colonial nature quoted from an art that was remote and probably irrelevant.

In the epigraph to *The Boys in the Island*, Christopher Koch cites Keats's description of the poet as 'a dreaming thing', bereft because he is an outcast from 'the great world'. Boys and girls in the island used to dream of leaving it; the great world began in Melbourne—or perhaps in Port Melbourne, where an ocean liner took us off to the northern hemisphere. Marking time in Hobart, we did our dreaming by absorbing the few works of art available to us. The art gallery and the public library used to be on opposite sides of the same block on Argyle Street, and the stop at which I caught the bus back to the suburbs was in between them under the sandstone wall of the Town Hall; thanks to the paintings I gazed at and the books I borrowed, I always went home with dreams of deracination churning inside my head. I did my best to ignore Mount Wellington, because it reminded me of where I was actually living.

A poem by Vivian Smith and a passage in a novel by Helen Hodgman, both set in the Tasmanian Museum and Art Gallery, recall what it was like to be so sadly dependent on art that either told sanctimonious lies about our reality or else casually effaced it. Smith in 'At an Exhibition of Historical Paintings, Hobart' notices the falsehoods peddled by colonial painters. Mount Wellington is 'tentative, uncertain': not its fault, since its presence is hardly apologetic, but a consequence of the artist's fumbling. The hills beneath it are bland, and they recede too deferentially. Quaint natives squat in compliant attitudes, awaiting extinction. Paint cleans every brick in a pink terrace. Smith, introducing time into this untemporal idyll, fills in a history that the frames exclude. His poem ends by reflecting on 'the pathos of the past', though that pathos really belongs to the present, which is unable to maintain the grand, self-deceptive colonial fiction. The paintings studied by Hodgman's heroine in *Blue Skies* are less wan and wistful: she calls them 'brazen', and sees them as windows opening onto lushly vegetated landscapes of sensual allure. The fantasies they depict also mirror the contents of her own disturbed mind. A lagoon, with 'a pale white girl … reflected on the waters', hints at 'unknown slimy things' below its surface. This is Hodgman's Tasmania: under beaming skies, a dark and scary place. The heroine 'escaped to the next picture. And to the next. And so around the room.' But as for Koch's dreaming thing—a boy who gets to Melbourne but then comes back to Hobart—no escape is possible. Hodgman's character disappears into one of the paintings, and floats through the looking glass into a macabre mayhem.

Neither Smith nor Hodgman are satisfied by what they find in the Hobart gallery. They know it is not the Louvre or the Uffizi, which is why they describe it so ironically. But Smith's touchingly proud urban documents and Hodgman's mawkishly sinister pre-Raphaelite dreams disclose art's ideal or devious ambitions— its alternate white and black magics. On the one hand, art honours reality. The stretched amplitude of the mountain and the harbour remind Smith of 'a grand gesture with wide-open arms', embracing the world. On the other hand, art revises or subverts a reality that was never more than an illusion, and peels the protective covering off the world. The women in the paintings look to Hodgman 'like shell-less crabs, edging … through Eden to

Thirty-six Views of Mount Wellington

destruction' (although, because art's techniques are indirect and sneaky, they travel not backwards but 'sideways, through one picture and into the next'). For Smith, in another poem, Tasmania is 'watercolour country'—soft, diluted, dissolving as if into tears, naturally elegiac. For Hodgman its tones are 'rich, glittering', like acrylic paint. The sun, if bright enough, dazes rather than illuminates; the real, violently intensified, curdles into surrealism. Between these two options, art's interpretation of Tasmania develops. The aims are contradictory, which is why we need those multiple views of Mount Wellington that I am going to describe.

The idea of enumerating views of the mountain is not mine. It comes from Vivian Smith's poem 'In the Grounds of the Old University, Hobart', and I purloin it because I think that art's reading of nature is a collaborative process, a pooling of intelligence and imagination. Smith himself, after all, took over the notion from Hokusai, who compiled an album with varying views of Mount Fuji. ('The Great Wave', referred to by Hughes in his account of Norfolk Island, comes from this collection: Hokusai aligns the surf on the breaking wave with the white conical peak of the distant mountain.) But Hokusai managed thirty-six views of Fuji, whereas Smith—typically modest, which is an endearing Tasmanian trait—says that he once dreamed of finding 'thirty ways of looking at its face'. He admits that it possesses a hundred faces which alter according to your viewpoint, while it also 'changes colour through the day'. Even so, he only manages two quick verbal sketches, calling it 'a mountain like a lion or a sphinx'. The set is not completed because the subject remains ambiguous, problematic:

> Mount Wellington has not yet been declared
> one of the sacred mountains of the world.

Smith allies it with other peaks on which gods dwell and salutes it as 'my Athos and my Ararat,/ my Fuji', but if you climb it you find no shrine, only an 'extinct volcanic site half blown away'—although, since the mountain has acquired some extra jewellery in the years since Smith looked at it as a student on the Domain campus, you now also come across the telecommunications masts that connect this great obstinate monolith with the chattering, echoing emptiness of outer space.

Smith excuses himself from the task of conferring sanctity on the mountain: 'if this had been Japan' he might have compiled an anthology like Hokusai's, but it isn't so he does not. Of course he could not be expected to, since a religion has to accrete through the centuries, slowly eliciting common consent. But in a way, though it's not the purpose of the poem to notice this, that is what has happened in Tasmania, thanks to the visual and verbal artists who have made Mount Wellington a cult object. Everyone in Japan worships Fuji, though the convergence of so many pilgrims has desanctified it: the crowded trails to the top are like zigzagging extensions of the escalators on the Tokyo subway, and the queues of climbers litter the volcanic rock with wrappings from their cans of film. Our religion may be unofficial, but it is more genuinely reverent. Here there is still room for individuals to stand alone and gape up at this astounding giant. You know that people feel a religious awe about Mount Wellington because they express it in a characteristically Australian way by swearing at it. I remember a student friend of mine suddenly stopping in his tracks in the centre of town—actually in the middle of the street, since we were on a protest march against the Vietnam war at the time—and exclaiming 'Bloody hell, just look at that flaming thing!' It was in its way as lyrical a response as Richard Flanagan's when he ranges across the adjectival spectrum in *Death of a River Guide* to describe 'the immense aqua presence of the mountain behind Hobart, lined at its summit by apricot clouds'. My mate coloured the mountain with some more expletives, riper than Flanagan's apricots, but I had better not put them back into his mouth: he is a respectable public servant these days. I was startled by his reaction, because it was so unlike him. It was as if he had got down on his knees to Mount Wellington there and then. Flanagan himself addresses the mountain with the same abusive fervency in the essay he wrote to introduce Peter Dombrovskis's collected photographs of it. Here he calls Mount Wellington a 'big blasted bastard of rock'. I was going to say that this time he'd abandoned poetic prose, but you'll notice the alliteration.

The colonists who imposed a map of their own remote home on this new country had trouble sanctifying Mount Wellington. John West in the *History of Tasmania* he wrote in 1852 quoted

Wordsworth's 'Sonnet to the Derwent', which blessed his own benign native landscape in the north of England: 'Among the mountains were we nursed, loved stream!' The sentiment suited Cumberland, where the peaks are rounder, mammary-like, but Tasmania repudiated this mild Anglican worship of nature. Marcus Clarke thought that our rugged mountains had a 'contemptuous grandeur' because they mocked the 'trim utilitarian civilisation' at their base. Louisa Ann Meredith, in the book about her Tasmanian home that she published in the same year as West's history, managed to reconcile herself to the Tasmanian Alps by fusing them with the memory of European feudalism. She describes a 'lofty expanse of crag, and battlement, and peak', as if not sure whether what she is looking at is raw rock or stone moulded into a feudal castle. What she calls 'the Tasmanian Ben Lomond', an imitator of the northern original, is her 'new mountain friend'. But she condescends to befriend Ben because he belongs to a social class with which she can be on visiting terms: the personified pinnacle is 'the lordly chief of a great mountain group on the north-east of our beautiful island'. Darwin likewise, on his ascent of Mount Wellington in 1836, complained about 'the thickness of the wood' and its damp, rotting luxuriance. Nature was only tolerable if it mimicked the polite deportment of society: the eucalypts arranged themselves into 'a noble forest', and the tree ferns opened 'elegant parasols' like ladies promenading in a London park. On the summit he complacently surveyed the 'tame outline' of the adjacent range, and was pleased that the estuary could be 'mapped with clearness': cartography assumes a divine perspective.

The watercolourist Skinner Prout, visiting in the 1840s, reduced the mountain to lovability by rusticating it. As he represents it, the pinnacle is smoothed, rounded, then pushed back to a convenient distance; despite the gaunt, fire-blackened tree trunks, the foreground of Prout's scene unpacks some evidence of Clarke's trim utilitarian civilisation. The old woman with her basket might be waiting for a bus, and the family in the hut behind her keep chooks, as my parents used to do in our backyard during the 1950s. The cabin's smoking chimney vouches for its cosiness and proves that the mountain is habitable. Prout's Tasmanian views recede into wildness, but the area closest to us is always cleared, settled, whether by the humpy that shelters an Aboriginal family and their dog in 'Native Encampment' or by Lady Jane Franklin's optimistic little temple. In 'Our Tasmanian Home', Mount Wellington retreats to a far corner of the horizontal view; the subject is Prout's house on Macquarie Street, shaded by an obliging tunnel of trees.

At least John Glover resisted the domesticating metaphors which saw mountains as battlemented castles or ferns as feminine umbrellas. Glover daringly reversed the terms of such comparisons when, after painting the dances at a corroboree, he declared that he found 'more enjoyment and Mirth in such occasions than I ever saw in a Ballroom in England'. Appropriately enough, it was Glover who first saw sanctity in Mount Wellington. Smith mentions Athos, Ararat and Fuji as divine citadels, but the mountain everyone regards as the anteroom of heaven is Olympus, where the quarrelsome, adulterous Greek gods dwelt. Glover painted Mount Olympus in 1813. A modern turbaned Greek in a twilit foreground points towards the peak, though neither he nor his companions look at it. Perhaps they know better than to gaze directly at the home of deity; more likely, they take Olympus for granted and have an amused scepticism about its myths. Far off across a plain, the sunlit peak is crowned or wreathed with cloud. To the romantic eye, divinity evaporates: the cloud marks the self-effacement of a creator who merges with nature.

Twenty years later, soon after his emigration to Van Diemen's Land, Glover took a closer look at an Olympian mountain in a painting he made at Kangaroo Point, across the harbour from the centre of Hobart. Now the decorous, static Greeks have been replaced by the Aboriginal tribes who cavort around a fire or splash in the water, relishing the two opposed elements and celebrating the vital energy of nature. And over the silvery harbour, above the golden foothills, stands the sacred peak, its brow honorifically fringed by cloud, like Glover's Olympus. The bottom half of the painting acknowledges a clash between cultures. The Aborigines, playing out their doomed revels in the shadows, are lined up against the masts and spires and towers of Hobart. The town, depopulated and inert, stores commodities in its warehouses and barracks; it cannot match the animated delight of the dancers, the swimmers and the eurhythmic trees on Kangaroo Point, but all the same it is graced by a band of brightness. The harbour marks an uneasy, disputed frontier. Once the eye passes the horizon that is set halfway up the canvas—or, to paraphrase the Bible, after we lift up our eyes up to the hills—this stand-off becomes irrelevant. A cleft of darkness at the peak singles out Mount Wellington and detaches it from the rest of the range; it expands into a sky larger than that above Olympus, and the clouds that seethe from it, as if just exhaled by its wet valleys after a downpour, look like the thoughts of whichever god lives up there.

The rock seems sentient, intelligent. The dotted pointilism with which Glover applied the paint here breaks down Mount Wellington's mineral rigidity and gives its furry flanks the texture and the tone of warm, veined, pulsing flesh. The painter Edith Holmes told Vivian Smith that 'For me the mountain has a human face'. Smith notes in his poem about her that Holmes travelled to Paris so she could learn how to see Mount Direction. She went, presumably, to study Cézanne's paintings of Mont Sainte-Victoire, but she refused to learn his lesson, which was that of abstraction. Cézanne saw his mountain abstractly, as an assemblage of those cubes and triangles that for Plato's Timaeus were the constituents of nature. When Edith Holmes came back to gaze again on her mountains, she did not reduce them to geometrical theorems. She defied the dehumanising vision of modernism, and insisted on recognising human features. I think the face that Glover paints is superhuman, which is why he can hardly risk more than a physiognomic hint. The creases beneath the summit are a furrowed forehead, worthy of Zeus or Jehovah. The mountain may be Olympian, yet it is also the kind of mountain that Moses climbed in quest of revelation.

The classical analogy is natural enough, since Tasmania possesses a Mount Olympus of its own, which WC Piguenit—who crossed Lake St Clair in a boat to get a better view—painted in 1875 and identified as 'the Source of the Derwent'. Piguenit called the mountain 'majestic'. It's a shame that it has to be flattered by invoking the ranks of nobility and monarchy, as if such heights existed only to be the thrones for gods, kings or generals like Wellington, but the meteorological drama concocted by Piguenit tries to manifest exaltation as well as grandeur or majesty. Purple mists blur the rough, forested slopes; then the ridge, jaggedly upright, thrusts itself into the sky, its incisors of rock cutting through the undergrowth so that we seem to be looking at a sudden evolutionary spurt, a second creation. Dark clouds boil above it, as in Glover's view of Mount Wellington, though further off the sky is blindingly bright. The membrane may be about to become transparent, showing us what lies on the other side.

It's fascinating to compare Glover's view from Kangaroo Point with Piguenit's 1884 painting 'Mount Wellington from Kangaroo Bay'. The difference between them indicates how art alters nature, and shows too how malleable the mountain is. Piguenit manipulates the perspective to make the mountain steeper, and tugs a bank of clouds down to the foothills so that the summit can float above it, apparently unanchored; the Organ Pipes are also elongated, and directly catch the rising sun in a benediction; the clouds are molten gold, and they seem to bubble up from some gulf that lies just behind the mountain, making the rock look airy, depthless and illusory. Exactly fifty years separate the two paintings, but much has changed in the lower halves of the compositions, which document the crouched town. The dancing, swimming Aborigines have been cleared away; the point on which they had their campfire is itself eliminated by Piguenit, who places himself in the middle of the bay. He might almost have been censoring Glover's painting, cutting out the shore that still belonged to its earliest inhabitants. The wading fishers with their spears have been supplanted by men in boats, interested not in subsistence but in a catch to sell at the wharf. Jetties protrude into the bay, as if the two shores were reaching out towards each other, with human intervention striving to close the gap left by nature. The white church steeples picked out by Glover are replaced by factory chimneys, whose smoke challenges the misty flurries in the sky.

In heaven there is glory; on earth there is industry. The juxtaposition suggests a kind of complicity: the dynamism that excited the Romantics when they described nature—the creative ferment Piguenit saw in the King William Range, which looked to him 'like huge billows from a stormy sea'—was harnessed by dynamos and turbines, transformed into the steam or electricity that ran engines. Piguenit's Mount Wellington may look Olympian, but he was enough of a scientist to be able to analyse the valuable minerals that made up the Tasmanian bedrock. In a lecture to a meeting of the Australian Association for the Advancement of Science in Hobart in 1892, he quoted the surveyor James Scott, with whom he had travelled to Port Davey. The land, Scott said, was 'destitute of timber', but the mountains made up for it, 'being of quartzite or some silicious stone'. In *Paradise Lost* it is God who makes the earth, but the devils who ravage it in quest of minerals, accidentally setting off a nitrous explosion. God creates nature, which enables men (or fallen angels) to discover gunpowder, another motor and motive force of human history. In a painting of the Derwent estuary, Knut Bull placed a quarry on the Domain in the foreground, to emphasise the way industrious man was gorging on the earth and leaving bite marks. Pantheism shook hands with profiteering. The landscapes painted by the Romantics assuaged the consciences of city-dwellers who were ravaging the countryside; they atoned for the brutal indifference to nature that produced the industrial economy. For me as a boy, the truly sublime spectacle was not the mountain but the zinc works, pestilentially fuming all night long on the scabrous hills of suburban Lutana: here were my 'satanic mills'.

In Henry Gritten's 1856 view of Hobart Town, there's a preview of the way the competition between nature and economic nurture was developing. Mount Wellington with its snow cap now looks elderly, grey. It retires into the sky rather than rearing up; a white haze almost blots it out. Down below, Gritten—whose viewpoint places him closer to the settlement than Glover or Piguenit, because he wants to enumerate its man-made bounty—examines human activity, set against the mountain's weary inertia. There are more ships than ever in the harbour, and from one of them a steer is being cumbrously unloaded. The delinquent God who created the southern hemisphere failed to provision it adequately, so the colonists had to import the species that were expected to increase and multiply: cattle in this case, but also the sheep and rabbits that reduced large sections of the mainland to a gnawed desert. The white steeple of St David's, always used as the still point in a busily turning world by Glover, continues to occupy its mound, but over on Battery Point it has a rival. Beside the tower of St George's stands a windmill, energetically making the air turn a profit, and on its vanes Gritten superimposes the masts of the largest ship. Its sails are furled, but that only makes the diagram neater: the X of the windmill has the same shape as the cruciform rigging, though tilted at an angle. Like Calvary, the ship supports three crosses. The middle one is the tallest, almost presuming to overtop the purple slope of the mountain. For the convicts, Van Diemen's Land was literally a place of excruciation, which is why Porter in *The Tilted Cross* sees the Organ Pipes as 'gallows and crucifixes of fused snow', rhyming with the gibbet erected in the centre of town. Porter's crosses poke into a sky unpatrolled by angels. Gritten's image lacks this angry atheism; on land and shore his mercantile crosses grow upwards as unstoppably as New York skyscrapers, confident that no superior power will debar them. It's no wonder that the mountain looks white and fatigued, ready to be absorbed by the pallid sky. God is dying.

In the same year as Gritten's watercolour, Knut Bull painted his 'Entrance to the River Derwent from the Springs, Mount Wellington', for which I have a sickly weakness. Prout in the previous decade had done his best to develop a homely empathy with the landscape; Bull, however, looks away from the town at the base of the mountain and follows the river towards the cold ocean into which it pours. Glover's sun, in paintings like 'My Harvest Home', represents fertility, and also serves as the bright eye of a benign, supervising deity. In a letter from Mills' Plains in 1833, his son reported on a bountiful harvest of wheat and thanked 'Goodness', looking forward to the rising price it would fetch; Glover too equated gold sunbeams with a pile of gold coins, and saw both as manifestations of God's grace. Bull's sun is rising, but with no promise of ripeness and riches. Its first beams scorch a stretch of dense jungle and stain the sky; the only witnesses of the daybreak are two birds, one hunched and miserable like a dyspeptic vulture, the other more spry although it has chosen to perch on a leafless, skeletal tree. A few plumes of smoke rise from the bush—marking the chimneys of cosy homesteads like Prout's cabin on Mount Wellington, or the simmering remains of a holocaust that has left the land uninhabited all over again? Bull's dawn really ought to be a final sunset, seen from the viewpoint of that favourite Romantic character, the last man left alive on our planet, painted by John Martin and described in a futuristic novel about the extinction of the human race by Mary Shelley. The monopolistic ego has inherited the earth, which could be why I like this painting so much: the only child is a born solipsist.

Bull's painting suggests that you can find the entire history of humanity in microcosmic Tasmania—and, with Darwin's help, you can even localise that history on Mount Wellington. Glover once sketched an Aboriginal couple as Adam and Eve, observed by a serpent which was probably not demonised by their less guilt-ridden mythology. His biblical narrative of mankind's early travails in this promised land is extended in 'Mountain Wellington with Orphan Asylum'. Vivian Smith complained that our mountain wasn't as holy as Ararat, on which Noah moored his ark as the flood waters began to drain. But in Glover's painting, Mount Wellington actually is Ararat, and the rainbow writes a new covenant across the fresh sky, protecting the asylum inside an iridescent dome and rescuing us all from our godless, existentially orphaned condition. The 'Sacred Theory of the Earth', promulgated in the seventeenth century by Bishop Burnet, conjectured that our world before Noah's flood was a flat verdant plain, and attributed mountains to the turbulence of that first catastrophe, when earth was swallowed by the abyss, swilled round in chaos and violently regurgitated. Burnet's allegorical geology was remembered by Wordsworth and Coleridge; perhaps Glover also knew of it, although here he contradicts its fatalism. The green mountain might have just emerged from beneath the water. Its contours are still malleable, no more rigid than the ephemeral clouds or the brief shimmering arc of light.

In certain moods, Mount Wellington does seem to liquefy: in *The Doubleman*, Christopher Koch's hero—ritually farewelling Tasmania—stands on the Domain at sunset looking towards it across the valleys that contain Hobart's suburbs, and feels its 'blue and violet' expanse to be 'deep as fathoms of water', which he is tempted to dive into. The ocean, or the oceanic consciousness, has not retreated, and it here engulfs Mount Wellington all over again. Koch's hero believes he is watching 'some vast process of transfiguration'. For Glover, a similar scene shows the earth being moulded into form—closer to Genesis than to the tumult described by Burnet after the deluge, when 'indigested heaps of stone' were vomited up to form mountains. The trees in the foreground have the 'trilling and graceful play' that is Glover's signature: they bend sideways to get a better view of the divine events, and like an ecstatic congregation seem to be dancing for joy. They see, as God complacently remarks about his handiwork in Genesis, that it is good. For Glover, Tasmania is Eden. For Bull, it looks more like Armageddon. His view points towards the far south-west, where the chipped basalt columns that protrude from the ocean and the carious cliffs really do look—if you see them from the air—like the products of some recent tantrum by a destructive creator.

The summit of a mountain suits the mystic because it offers glimpses of supernature. But below, in the mountain's shadow, a more psychological drama rages. During the 1750s Edmund Burke's essay on the twin categories of the sublime and the beautiful taught the Romantics how to respond to landscape, and eventually influenced the first accounts of Tasmanian scenery; Burke suggested that our reactions to the countryside around us stirred up again our earliest and most potent emotions, initially prompted by our parents. The mother is a loving, protecting figure, whom we associate with the kind of nature we call beautiful—shady dells, banks of flowers, purling streams, all the cocooning spaces of literary pastoral. The father is a larger, remoter, more threatening presence. We find traces of him in nature's sublime phenomena, which are alarming because so overpowering—thunderstorms, angry seas, and of course mountains. Beauty, with its sensual appeal, entices us to reproduce ourselves; sublimity teaches us to preserve ourselves by making war on our oppressors. We can choose between female comfort and male violence. I have to acknowledge that Mount Wellington, for me, was a father-fixation. For this very reason I appreciate and envy the way that Richard Flanagan feminises the mountain. In *Death of a River Guide*, he sees it rising behind the town that is its 'offspring' and likens it to 'a crabby matriarch ready to strike out at anybody who badmouthed her child'. By changing the mountain's gender, he reclassifies it as beautiful not sublime, and his image of the mother defending her brood legitimises its menace. If I had been able to see Mount Wellington like this, my personality and my style might have been very different. Flanagan accuses me of matricide, a wounding rejection of the motherland. He may have picked the wrong parent. It's the complementary crime that I was guilty of, at least in my imagination, and I committed it whenever I described the mountain.

In his novel, Flanagan attributes that adoring filial attitude to a character. His pinioned, drowning narrator hangs suspended between life and death like the sculptural cut-outs of steel that line a fence on Molle Street in Hobart, 'simultaneously in agony and knowledge' as they raise tormented arms towards the mountain, which they address as their saviour. In his ecological essay Flanagan is more indirect. I am intrigued by the shy way he says that he doesn't want to pretend that Mount Wellington is 'some sort of holy place', after which he instantly adds that 'for some people—and maybe I am even among them—it is that'. The Romantic worship of mountains gave the world a verticality it previously lacked, and suggested that the sky might be more than a painted ceiling. Telescopes enabled men to scrutinise infinitude, but from a distance; mountains were arduous step-ladders, inviting us to clamber closer to it. It's true that mountain-climbing is not exactly a reliable school of morals. Nietzsche's Zarathustra scampers on the heights and vaults over abysses. Hitler built himself an eyrie, called the Eagle's Nest, on a dizzy precipice outside Salzburg. But anyone with a clear head will resist feeling that he has triumphed over the mountain and is somehow greater than it. Instead, the ascent—as I remember from my own half-dozen trips to the top of Mount Wellington—is humbling, chastening. The sublime is not supposed to aggrandise us; by measuring a puny individual against the ferocity of the elements, it points out how small we are.

Australian nature, so often hard-bitten and deadly, never prompted the messianic patriotism that made American painters exult when they first saw the Hudson Valley or Niagara Falls or the Grand Canyon or Yosemite. Our explorers took a bitter pleasure in pointing out nature's sterility, which is why a dry stretch of boulders resembling clods near the summit of Mount Wellington was nicknamed 'the ploughed field'. Lloyd Rees's lithograph of 'The Pinnacles, Mount Wellington' is small and therefore an antidote to gigantism, but by closely scrutinising details it finds a resurgent energy in the dead volcano: the boulders are thrusting thumbs or grasping fingers, and the bush growing sideways testifies to the battling resilience of plants stranded above the tree line. Rees makes visible the struggle of life in all its forms. Rain suits the lithographic process, because it etches channels and digs into the sky like scratching claws as it falls. The image was made in 1980 when Rees was eighty-five, and perhaps it finds in Mount Wellington an emblem of old age and its austere, wintry endurance. Glover painted the mountain sappily clad in green, like an extension of the market gardens in the foothills. For Rees, its bones show through.

He declined to present nature as a church, which was the instinctive response of American painters. The standing stones are not formed into a mystifying cromlech, and the Organ Pipes do not play a Bach partita. Robert Emerson Curtis, however, in the ink drawing of Hobart and its attractions that he made in 1936, took the metaphor literally, turned the cracked piles of rock into actual metallic organ pipes, and even sat an organist at an imaginary console beneath them—a figure with the long white mane and enraptured air of Franz Liszt, who pedals away and makes the mountain exhale what I take to be a great jubilant chord of C major. The truth is that the closer you get to the Organ Pipes, the less convincing the metaphoric resemblance is. On weekends during his schooldays, Vivian Smith used to go on rambles through South Hobart, and at the top of a fern gully he remembers being 'rewarded with a side view of the Organ Pipes which looked huge and frightening and barbaric': not at all the piece of Anglican church furniture the name intended. It's interesting that Smith calls the sidelong view his reward, despite the fright it gave him. It was an artistic gift, because art recreates the familiar world by seeing it from a personal, particular angle.

If the Organ Pipes are an altar, they do indeed suggest, like the Aztec pyramids in Mexico, that a faith more atavistic than Christianity celebrates its rites up there. The savage grandeur of the place is best caught in a huge photographic collage by David

Thirty-six Views of Mount Wellington

Stephenson, which belongs to the National Gallery of Australia in Canberra—a horizontal assemblage of fifteen enormous, overlapping images, glued together like the fused rock itself, so large that when I went to see it in the shed outside Canberra where it is stored, it had to be painfully removed from an upper shelf by a fork-lift truck. The spars of stone in the photograph are like razory incisors; a gap opens as if this were a hungry mouth, ready to gobble up the dead timber on the slope below. Stephenson calls his massive, heavy construction a self-portrait, even though he is scarcely visible in the shadows. The young Smith heard tell of walkers vanishing in the bush on the mountain, which to him intensified its alarming mystique. Stephenson has sentenced himself to that fate, and disappears into his own photograph. Hardly visible in the shadows, he stands on a ledge of the Organ Pipes like a skinny Gothic carving in a niche; if the exposure had taken longer, he might have petrified. Though Stephenson is an American who now lives on Mount Wellington, he has not brought with him to Australia the sense of nature as an alfresco cathedral that extends through American art from Thomas Cole's paintings to the photographs of Ansel Adams and Eliot Porter. The mountain's starkness rebuts this easy theology.

Much as I admire Stephenson's tragic, gravely witty panorama, I can hardly allow an expatriate American the last word on our mountain. I'll end with Peter Dombrovskis, whose photographs of the mountain were published shortly after his death in 1996, and were introduced by Flanagan's essay. The book is called *On the Mountain*, which is a reminder that most colonial views look up at the mountain from the middle of the city or from the harbour and see it as if through a picture window. The first image in Dombrovskis's sequence shows how little you know about the mountain if you spend your life at the base of it. Hobart here is obliterated by low cloud. On such a day, we customarily say that the mountain has gone missing: an arrogant, self-centred error, since it's our town that has been expunged. Down below, the day must have been overcast. On the heights the sun is shining, and it turns the clouds to burnt gold. The vista is Olympian, and because we think of the classical gods as enlargements of ourselves there's a certain anthropomorphism to it: the Van Diemen Buttress is a family group of rocks, and the two poised boulders on the right loll together like two heads affectionately resting on one another. Nothing could be less like the saw-toothed Organ Pipes of Stephenson. Yet it's typical of Dombrovskis to see more than a trinity of Henry Moore monoliths. What most strikes me is his sharp, deft focusing on the plants that have managed to put down roots in a crevice between the clumps of rock.

The familiar profile of Mount Wellington is visible only to lowlanders. If you are up on top of it, like Dombrovskis, you can't see it as a whole; indeed that there is no whole, since the mountain is an entire range. Therefore the only way to understand it is to study its parts, which are also puzzlingly contradictory. Its vegetation is tropically damp at Fern Tree, though by the time you get to the summit it becomes bleak and dessicated. The lower slopes are lush; the peak is alpine. Dombrovskis concentrates on beautiful details—tiny everlasting daisies, delicate fingery fern fronds, the budding Richea dracophylla from which life seethes in impatient jutting nodes of new growth—not sublime enormities. This preference marks a choice of gender: for him as for Flanagan, the mountain is not a grumpy patriarch. With its cool streams, it is as riverine as the female body. Its textures are yielding, porous, seldom harsh: hence the cliffs of sandstone like the one nicknamed Sphinx Rock, or the cushion plant, which is an overstuffed armchair made of moss. The most maternal image he finds on the mountain is the nest of a blackbird balanced on a dry fern, with four blue eggs in its nursery of woven, masticated twigs.

The last image in *On the Mountain* balances the first. After a snowfall, the clouds have rolled back to leave the city clear; they congregate in the estuary, though beyond them you can see hilly ridges that float above the mist. A diagonal axis of vision aligns a small boulder in the foreground with the smaller, remoter tumulus of the Casino at Wrest Point. When Glover looked down at Hobart from the foothills, he always used the white spire of St David's as a point of orientation; the Casino—mercifully indistinct, though you can still see that it's leaning at an angle, ready to become a quaint romantic ruin like its predecessor in Pisa—inherits this function for Dombrovskis. But the eye only pauses there, and then travels onwards to the vaporous horizon. This visual itinerary reverses that of the colonial painters. Hobart is Mount Wellington's doormat; we are its background, not vice versa. Yet although the distances in Dombrovskis's image are sublime, the details near to us are beautiful. The tough, spiky grass is invigorated by the cold, and the narrow slice of sunlight that begins to thaw them is as beatific as Glover's rainbow.

I promised thirty-six views of Mount Wellington. Though I haven't been counting, I know I have fallen short of the total. The list, however, is open-ended, and I leave others to add to it, in words or images or perhaps music: someone should write a concerto for the soloist whom Robert Emerson Curtis installed at the Organ Pipes. Potentially, the views of Mount Wellington are numberless. Reality depends on our perceptions of it, and is amplified by those layered, superimposed responses. Though we share the earth, each person's experience of it is unique; the world is renewed when—thanks to imagination, the most miraculous of mental faculties—we see it through someone else's eyes. As Proust said, 'The pleasure that an artist gives is to make us know another universe.' We are at last discovering Tasmania's universality.

acknowledgments

My thanks to Donald McDonald, Chairman of the ABC, for offering me the chance to deliver the 2004 Boyer Lectures, to my producer Janne Ryan for her incisive commentary on the texts and her advice during the recordings, and to Jenny Parsonage for policing my pronunciation. Mae Gannon and Nick Bron made expert arrangements for my trip to Sydney to tape the broadcasts; I am grateful as well to Susan Morris-Yates, who helped me cross the gap between talk and print.